A CRY FOR HELP

*One Veteran's Battle with the
Army Awards Branch
to Recognize the Men and Women
Who Fought for Our Country*

BEN R. GAMES, PH D

©Copyright, 2012, Ben R. Games, PhD

All Rights Reserved
No part of this book maybe reproduced, stored in a retrieval system, or transmitted by any means. This includes electronic, mechanical, photocopying, recording, or other means.
Without the written permission of the author.

ISBN: 978-1-60414-622-6

**DEDICATED
TO
THE MEN & WOMEN
WHO WORK IN THE SHADOWS**

*ESPECIALLY TO THOSE AMERICANS WHO
VOLUNTEERED TO FLY WITH THE AUTHOR
AND WERE WOUNDED*
lived, and died under the "Warrior's Code"

Many military veterans during the Vietnam War did not know that some of their missions were classified and served to make the world a better place.

They are all heroes and part of America's history.

A "Special Thanks" to Harry Alexander, OSS, who taught the author about the need for gathering foreign intelligence and how to drop below the radar. God Bless

Ben R. Games, PhD

the men and women who work in the Shadows to help keep America free from Terrorist and the Dark Forces.

History is a window that looks into the future.

A copy of US Army Special Orders, newspaper reports, letters, and photographs are in the archives of the Historical Service Division, Department of the Army, Carlisle Barracks, Pa.. Copies of the DA Form 759 and AF Form 5 Flight Records are held for the VA by the Bay Pines, VFW, Veterans Service Office, Department of Florida, St. Petersburg, Florida. The official medical records of combat injuries were provided by the individual warriors for this historical report. Some records were sanitized to protect the men and women who work in the shadows. Releases signed by:

Ben R. Games, PhD, Major (USAF & Army)

David L. Walker, E-5 25th Infantry Division.

Joseph B. Kelly, (CIA Contract Officer), USAF Ret.

TABLE OF CONTENTS

DEDICATION	3
AUTHOR'S BIO	6
THE GUARDIAN ANGEL	10
THE CONSPIRACY TO CHANGE HISTORY	16
STATEMENT	17
CONSPIRACY FACTS	28
PROLOGUE	46
HISTORICAL DOCUMENTS	57
A VFW BIOGRAPHY	69
RICHES	78
FUUJIN	185
FUUJIN & THE 4TH FIGHTER SQUADRON	187
SHANGRI-LA VIETNAM	216
AUTHORS PERSONAL INFORMATION	220

AUTHOR'S BIO

Ben R. Games, PhD, Major, CW-4, TCNA-6

Holds the degrees; Doctor of Philosophy (PhD), Business Administration, Pacific Western University; BS Degrees in; Science, PWU; Nuclear Energy, Air University; Nuclear Disaster Operational Control, USAF; Electronic Engineering, Keio University; Geo-Economics, Notre Dame University; Aviation Pilot Training, Class 43K; Jet Fighter Pilot training, USAF; Radar Navigation training, Victorville AFB; Bombardier School, San Angelo Army Air Field, and Aircraft Accident Investigations, Norton AFB.

Certified Teacher; Basic Flight Training Randolph Field, US Army Air Forces; Instrument Instructor, Texas A&M; Superintendent of Basic Math School, Kessler AFB; Radar Maintenance School, Biloxi, Mississippi; Licensed Insurance Agent IN64, Airport Manager MI

83-17, Accounting BSc, and Public Health Pest Control FL 1038.

The author has served on the Board of Directors of the Turks and Cacios National Airlines Inc; H. Jobero Inc an investment firm; Amsie Ltd LLC a building and investment company; Valley Mobilehome Association Inc; Indiana Air Safety Board; and Sabre Service Corporation a legal firm. He co-authored a paper presented to the Aero Medical Lab at Wright Field on the use of pressures instead of vacuums for astronaut training. His doctorate dissertation was on Employer and Employee Relationships Controlled by Governments.

His professional publications included the 1950 secret operational plan for the air defense of the United States, Employee Leasing, Payroll Credit Plan, and Fax/Accounting. He started writing a news column in the Elkhart High School paper in 1942 and continued in 1943 as editor of "Solo" the US Army Primary Class Book of 43K. Novels include *My Guardian Angel,* an autobiography, (2001), *Beyond* (2003), *Galaxy Slaves* (2009) fiction, *Without Prejudice* (2003), and *Jihad Vietnam*, nonfiction (2008).

TO OBTAIN RELEASE OF DOCUMENTS AND PHOTOS FROM "THE CONSPIRACY TO CHANGE HISTORY" TEXTBOOK

To obtain a release or permission to use, copy, or reproduce the pictures, letters, and works of the author; Ben R. Games, PhD for the text book "The Conspiracy To Change History". Please phone Fideli Publishing Inc., 888-343-3542 and ask for Robin.

STEPS

1. *Purchase a Textbook direct from Fideli Publishing.*
2. *Furnish your name, address, and phone number.*
3. *FIRST FIFTY (50) ORDERS WILL RECEIVE A FREE "EL CAZADOR HALF REALE COIN."*

YOU WILL ALSO RECEIVE

- One text book stamped; Permission to quote; copy documents & pictures.

- One Genuine Half Silver Reale coin from the El Cazador that changed the world to indicate that you have a Fideli Release.

By the middle of the 1700s, the vast wealth produced by the silver mines of Mexico had become the pride of the Spanish Empire. The problem was how to convert tons of silver into a tradeable form. The massive silver Eight Reales was sought and valued through-out the world. In North America where 13 tiny colonies were struggling for survival it quickly became the unofficial coin of the land. President Thomas Jefferson convinced Congress to adopt the Eight Reales as legal tender of the United States. It remained legal tender until 1857, and today the colonies have become 50 states with a Federal Reserve Bank struggling under a massive debit. The Silver Reales may once again become part of the unofficial trading pardoner of the people.

OFFER MAY BE WITHDRAWN AT ANY TIME

THE GUARDIAN ANGEL
Ben R. Games, PhD

A young boy watched the birds fly and thought,
"Why can't I?"

Then in Sunday School he learned
that Angels fly and thought,
"Why can't I?"

A young man and woman holding hands stood looking up at the clouds in the sky and the woman said,
"Why don't we fly?"

Now the Lord has a plan for all his children. He looked down and saw that they were getting ahead of the plan. If something wasn't done there would be a traffic jam at the Pearly Gates.

He called the Archangel Michael and told him to think of ways to help the plan.

The Archangel formed a committee of Angels and told them that the Head Man had said to do something. They decided that every pilot must have a Guardian Angel to watch over him or her to see that he or she did not show up at the Pearly Gates before it was time.

Then the Archangel went back to the Lord. He told him about the Committee and their idea. Then he asked the Lord which Angel to assign to the task. The Lord sighed and looked again. There were so many trying to fly that one Angel would never do.

The Lord said, "These are my Children, so assign all the Angels who watch over the children to take turns watching over pilots."

So, it came to pass that every pilot was assigned a Guardian Angel to help see that they didn't get into heaven before their time.

Ben R. Games, PhD

Union Man In Helicopter Training

FT. RUCKER, ALA. — Army aviation operations in Vietnam so impressed a civilian helicopter pilot that he joined his home state National Guard and is now finishing UH-1 "Huey" Pilot Transition Training at Ft. Rucker's Lowe Field.

Warrant Officers, W-2 Ben R. Games of Union, Mich., and his wife, Helen, are both qualified civilian helicopter pilots and are one of the few such husband and wife helicopter pilot teams in the United States.

Also a fixed-wing pilot, WO Games counts among his airborne accomplishments a flight from Elkhart to London via the Arctic Region; a flight across the Pacific Ocean, and glider flying in Australia.

In February and March of last year, Mr. and Mrs. Games embarked on a dual-purpose tour of Vietnam. They traveled throughout South Vietnam to satisfy their curiosity about the struggle there and also visited their son, Navy Petty Officer Third Class Ben R. Games Jr., who was stationed in Vietnam.

And a promient part of their Vietnam tour was the opportunity to witness firsthand the work of Army aviators.

"I was so impressed with the Army's air operations in Vietnam that I decided I'd like to be a part of it," Games said.

Upon his return home, he offered his civilian flying experience to the Michigan Army National Guard, and he was promptly accepted. He was subsequently set here for initial Army aviation instruction.

The UH-1 transition training marks WO Games' second assignment to Ft. Rucker in the past year, and he hopes to receive further training here in the UH-47 "Chinook."

"Being an experienced civilian helicopter pilot, I thought I knew a bit about flying," he said, "but I was really impressed with Army aviation training."

Again referring to flight training here, he added, "There is nothing else like it. I think it's outstanding."

HUSBAND-WIFE TEAM — Mrs. Ben R. Games, of Union, Mich., sits at the controls of a UH-1 "Huey" helicopter at Lowe Field, Ft. Rucker, Ala., where her husband, Warrant Officer, W-2 Games, second from left, is completing UH-1 pilot transition training. At left is Warrant Officer, W-2 Robert L. Pinckney, instructor, and at right is Warrant Officer, W-2 Leo A. Travis of Sacramento, Calif. WO Travis and WO Games are two of the 26 pilots in the current UH-1 transition course.

A Cry for Help

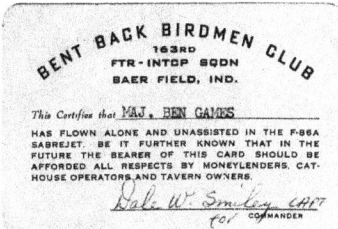

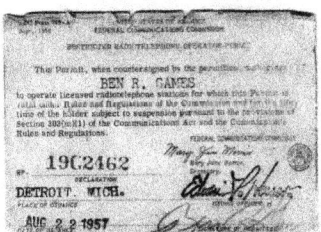

Ben R. Games, PhD

Manatee's Independent Newspaper   November 11-17, 2010   Volume 20 Edition 35

Ben Games (seated left) is shown in his favorite Army flight suit as he looks over some memorabilia of his 44 years in the Air Force and Army. With him is his wife, Helen, and David Walker, also of Ellenton, who holds the Bronze Star with Valor and met Games when he was rescued by him in Vietnam. Games' service stretched from WWII to Vietnam and he was involved in many classified military special operations.

Ellenton man served 44 years in military

(Editor's Note—the North River News today salutes all of our War veterans for their sacrifice on behalf of our country and its people. Although there are thousands of stories that could (and should) be recounted, we are telling the story of the long and unusual military career of a local man as a special salute to all our service personnel.)

BY CHARLES MILLER, New Writer

Meet Ben Games of Ellenton—fighter pilot, bomber pilot, helicopter pilot---veteran of World War II, Korea, the Berlin Airlift, the Cuban Missile Crisis and Vietnam. He's a PhD, the author of several books, and a lecturer.

He is also an activist working to get rights and benefits restored for many former servicemen and civilians who served as civilian employees of the CIA and contractors for the government in Vietnam.

Ben Games has a record of 44 years of continuous military service. He enlisted in the Army Air Corps in 1942 and served with it until the Air Force was formed in the late 1940s. During that time, his skill as a pilot put him in B-24 bombers and P-61 (Black Widow) night fighters in the Pacific Theater. He also made several special mission flights for the OSS.

Besides flying jet fighters, Games was assigned many special operations (highly classified) duties. One of the many highlights of his USAF career was when he served as a nuclear weapons officer in Europe during the Berlin Crisis. His other activities involving nuclear technology are classified.

He retired as a Major from the Air Force in 1967 after 20 years when he became concerned that his superiors might think he was too old to fly fighter planes and assign him a desk job.

So what does he do – he joins the Army as a helicopter pilot and served in Vietnam where he flew attack, counter-insurgency and rescue missions for Army Special Operations, assisting those men he is now trying to help. He retired from the Army after another 20 years of service in 1987.

Games thrived on flying and danger. He has been awarded the Distinguished Flying Cross for Heroism (he doesn't talk about it), the Bronze Star, 14 Air

VETERAN TO PAGE 5

A Cry for Help

_____ *VETERAN* FROM PAGE 1

Medals, two Legion of Merit Medals, the Army Commendation Medal and the American Defense Medal with three Stars. Additionally, he has received medals from other countries for his actions on their behalf.

During his military career, Games logged 737 combat missions and more than 20,000 hours as a pilot. His ID was "Gentle Ben."

At 87, Games is an imposing figure, especially when he's wearing his favorite outfit—an Army flight suit with a "Distinguished Flying Cross Club" emblem.

He and his wife, Helen, are natives of Elkhart County, Indiana, and have been married 67 years. They now live on a quiet street in Ellenton. They have two sons, Ben, Jr., who lives nearby and Jon, who is employed by the IRS and lives here in Florida. Their dog, Montana, also has a military ID.

But that's only part of the story. Ben, who has a Ph.D. in Business Administration from Pacific Western University, also was general manager of Turks and Caicos National Airline for a while.

Helen Games also has quite a record. She is an accomplished pilot and is "Whirlygirl #86"—because she was the 86th woman in the world to become a helicopter pilot. She accompanied her husband on many of his Army Special Operations assignments to dangerous places throughout the world. In fact, she was the first dependent to arrive at Johnson Air Force Base in Japan, the day after it surrendered, arriving from Okinawa.

In Vietnam, she also accompanied her husband at his various stations throughout the countryside. On one trip, she and Ben became "bait" for a Viet Cong tank attack that resulted in several enemy vehicles being destroyed.

Today, Ben's eyesight is slowly fading but he is still doing battle—this time with his own government. The issue—the denial of VA benefits and/or medals to wounded veterans who are listed as "unclassified" casualties—because they were rescued by units on secret missions. Other wounded veterans who receive full VA benefits are known as "historical" casualties.

Right now, Games is working with David Walker, an Ellenton businessman whom he once helped rescue. Walker, who made 27 combat assaults during his time in Vietnam, received the Bronze Star with Valor for his actions in defending a command bunker on New Year's Eve in 1968.

Even though Walker suffered wounds in Vietnam, when the helicopter in which he was riding was shot down, he never received the Purple Heart because he was listed as an "unclassified" casualty. The Purple Heart would make him eligible for additional VA benefits.

THE CONSPIRACY TO CHANGE HISTORY

STATEMENT of Ben R. Games, Ph.D.

www.FideliPublishing.com

This is a record of a Cyber Attack on the Veterans Administration's computer and the attempt to change history by the Military Awards Branch concerning the Vietnam War.

Editor: Robin Surface, BA. Fideli Publishing, Inc. Documents, pictures, and letters finished by the author, David Walker, BA, (Army), Helen M. Games, MBA., Joseph Kelly, CIA Contract Agent, (USAF ret).

STATEMENT

This information was taken from the author's Journals. Like all history recorded by official documents, it is subject to interpretation by the reader. This report was written to be read by researchers with no effort made to predetermine why or who would join a conspiracy to change the casualty lists of the Vietnam War.

Most citizen soldiers served in military units under commanders who were all subjected to the Articles of War and the US Military Code of Justice. There were also some soldiers who served in the shadows under a different set of rules. As the historic documents unfold, it will soon become a reading adventure which may make you believe that if the names were changed it could be "deja vu."

The information herein is based on the Games Clan's flying adventures during the Vietnam War. It is about flying Chinook CH-47 helicopters with "B" Company, "228" Aviation Battalion and aircraft of "E" Battery, "82" Artillery, 1st Cavalry Division. It is also about how the Games Clan lived and worked for their country during a time of world confusion. Ben and Helen lived on a Thai Firebase named Bear Cat while the author flew combat missions for Saigon Special Operations and snatch and grab missions for the CIA.

The author used the entries on his DD Form 759 flight records and notes written in his journal to conclude that a conspiracy to mislead the American people was being supported by the North Vietnamese during the "Paris Peace Talks."

History is the building blocks for a window looking into the future and once lived can never be changed. The author is not trying to change history, only to tell how his family lived in it. The saying "the future is not ours too see" is correct to a point. History has a habit of repeating itself, so if you don't like what has happened in the past, then you need to change the present. It's the only way.

The Vietnam War was fought with the US Secretary of State, North Vietnam, and United Nations establishing the rules of engagement. These rules were designed to give an advantage to the Chinese and North Vietnamese Communist soldiers who out numbered the Americans five to one. President Nixon and President Johnson had forgotten or chose to ignore that the Communists and fifty-seven Islamic Nations of the Brotherhood had gained control of the United Nations. During the Korean War, Berlin Crises, Vietnam War, and the Gulf Wars, the rules of combat were all designed for the United States military to lose the fight. This never happened, so the enemy started a battle to destroy the America People's Republic Form of Government from within.

The Enemy manipulate the value of peoples' expectations based on America's perception of reality. The Enemy uses word twisting and trickery around the clock to control the America citizens' understanding of the truth. The Vietnam War was a perfect test to see if the United States would give up the fight for freedom of the South Vietnamese people.

8 November 1969 Firefight at LZ Vivian Vietnam, 1st Cav. Div.

Aircraft Commander CW3 Ben R. Games

Ben R. Games, PhD

Awards made at LZ Bear Cat CH-47 Chinook Helicopter, "City of Elkhart"

Distinguished Flying Cross

A Cry for Help

Fighter Pilot Preserves Memories in Stories, Books & CDs

By Penny Fletcher
penny@observernews.net

Ben Games and his wife Helen met in the air and have spent much of their time looking down at the ground in the 66 years since that day.

"We were on a ride at a county fair in Elkhart, Indiana. One that used centrifugal force so that when we got high enough, the little seat we were in would completely flip over the top and come back around. My buddy and I were on leave from Ft. Lewis (Washington) and decided to take a ride in this loop-loop thing. There were four seats, and the girls (one of whom he later married) were in the two seats behind us."

The women had ridden bicycles to the fair, and Ben had his father's car, so the 17-year-old soldier volunteered to drive the girls home.

They dated only a short time before he returned to his base.

"When Helen graduated high school, she just took off and we got married. That was in 1942," he said. "Her parents didn't want her to leave so young and caught her the first time she tried to leave, so finally she just left without any clothes or anything."

She's now 84 and he's 85.

They've been married ever since. And what a full life they've had.

Ben was in the military for 35 years. He began in the Army Air Corps flying bombers and night fighters in World War II; transferred to the newly-organized Air Force and flew jet fighters in

Ben and Helen Games in 1942.

Ben and Helen Games today.

Photo Courtesy of Ben Games, Jr.

This CD contains the story of women pilots in World War II as told by Ben Games who served as an Army Acceptance Pilot for the last group of women pilots to be brought into the Army at the women's flight school. "At

Ben R. Games, PhD

DEPARTMENT OF THE ARMY
HEADQUARTERS 1ST CAVALRY DIVISION (AIRMOBILE)
APO San Francisco 96490

GENERAL ORDERS
NUMBER 8983

31 May 1970

AWARD OF THE BRONZE STAR MEDAL

1. TC 439. The following AWARDS are announced.

Awarded: Bronze Star Medal
Dates of service: As Indicated in Standard Name Line
Organization: Battery E, (Aviation), 82d Artillery
Theater: Republic of Vietnam
Authority: By direction of the President, under the provisions of Executive Order 11046, 24 August 1962.
Reason: For meritorious service, not involving participation in aerial flight, in connection with military operations against a hostile force in the Republic of Vietnam.

BOURGEOIS, JAMES L. 465680783 CAPTAIN ARMOR United States Army August 1969 to August 1970
SNYDER, DAVID M. 077365340 CAPTAIN FIELD ARTILLERY United States Army August 1969 to August 1970
EVANS, JOHN C. 267746988 FIRST LIEUTENANT FIELD ARTILLERY United States Army August 1969 to August 1970
SCHOBERT, PETER A. 060381402 FIRST LIEUTENANT FIELD ARTILLERY United States Army August 1969 to August 1970
GAMES, BEN R. 1165 CHIEF WARRANT OFFICER CW3 United States Army June 1969 to February 1970
RUMNEY, JOHN 041428681 WARRANT OFFICER WO1 United States Army August 1969 to August 1970
ELLIOT, PRESTON, H. 423586970 STAFF SERGEANT United States Army August 1969 to August 1970
ZAPREF, LUBEN K. 247704252 SPECIALIST SIX United States Army August 1969 to August 1970
WAYNE, LARRY L. 439703459 SERGEANT United States Army August 1969 to August 1970

FOR THE COMMANDER:

OFFICIAL:

Bruce B Bingham

BRUCE B. BINGHAM
1LT, AGC
Asst AG

E. C. MEYER
Colonel, GS
Chief of Staff

DISTRIBUTION:
2 - AG-ASD
90 - AVDAAG-AD
12 - AVDAAG-CR
6 - AVDAAG-R

SPECIAL DISTRIBUTION:
12 -TAGO, ATTN: AGPF-F
   (for official personnel files)
3 - AGPERSCEN, ATTN: AGPE-F
   Ft. Benjamin Harrison, Ind. 46216

A Cry for Help

DEPARTMENT OF THE ARMY
HEADQUARTERS 1ST CAVALRY DIVISION (AIRMOBILE)
APO San Francisco 96490

GENERAL ORDERS
NUMBER 718

13 January 1970

AWARD OF THE DISTINGUISHED FLYING CROSS

TC 439. The following AWARD is announced.

GAMES, BEN R. ...1165 CHIEF WARRANT OFFICER CW3 United States Army Company B, 228th Aviation Battalion (Assault Support Helicopter)(Airmobile)

Awarded: Distinguished Flying Cross
Date of action: 8 November 1969
Theater: Republic of Vietnam
Authority: By direction of the President, under the provisions of the Act of Congress, approved 2 July 1926
Reason: For heroism while participating in aerial flight evidenced by voluntary action above and beyond the call of duty in the Republic of Vietnam. Chief Warrant Officer Games distinguished himself by exceptionally valorous action on 8 November 1969, near Landing Zone Vivian, Republic of Vietnam. When on approach to the Landing Zone, the aircraft was struck by enemy fire which caused both engines to fail and ignited a fire. In spite of the hazardous conditions, he was able to cut off the fuel flow and assist the pilot in directing the craft away from populated areas. Although the ship was engulfed in flames, he remained on board until the crew had been evacuated. His outstanding flying ability and devotion to duty are in keeping with the highest traditions of the military service, and reflect great credit upon himself, his unit, and the United States Army.

FOR THE COMMANDER:

OFFICIAL:

BRUCE B. BINGHAM
1 LT, AGC
Asst AG

JOSEPH P. KINGSTON
Colonel, GS
Chief of Staff

DISTRIBUTION:
2 - AG-ASD
10 - AVDAAG-AD
2 - AVDAAG-OR
1 - G1
1 - AVDAAG-MPA

SPECIAL DISTRIBUTION:
2 - TAGO, ATTN: AGPF-F
  (for official personnel file)

LZ Vivian after Fire Fight on 8 Nov. 69 two of the enemy were VC working with regular North Vietnamese Army.

A Cry for Help

[Report of Separation from Active Duty — DD Form 214]

- Name: JAMES, BEN ROBERT
- Sex: M
- Social Security Number: 11165
- Date of Birth: Year 24 / Month 05 / Day 05
- Army/Component and Branch: ARNG MI
- Grade: CW4, Pay Grade: W-4
- Date of Rank: Year 76 / Month 07 / Day 03
- Selective Service Number: DNA
- Local Board Number: DNA
- Home of Record: 6445 Lake Sunrise Dr, Apollo Beach, FL 33570
- Station or Installation at which Effected: Fort Benjamin Harrison, Indiana 46216
- Type of Separation: RETIREMENT
- Effective Date: Year 77 / Month 12 / Day 31
- Character of Service: HONORABLE
- Type of Certificate Issued: DD Form 363A
- Command to Which Transferred: USAR Con Gp (RCPAC) 9700 Page Blvd St Louis, MO
- Last Duty Assignment and Major Command: HHD R&RO MI ARNG, LANSING, MI
- Place of Entry into Current Active Service: Lansing, MI 48913
- Date Entered Active Duty This Period: Year 73 / Month 07 / Day 02
- Terminal Date of Reserve: NA

Primary Specialty: 711A0 (760702) Unit Pers Tech — Related Civilian Occupation: NA
Secondary Specialty: 100B0 (690401) Helicopter Pilot — Related Civilian Occupation: NA

Record of Service:
	Years	Months	Days
(a) Net Active Service This Period	04	05	29
(b) Prior Active Service	16	04	21
(c) Total Active Service (a + b)	20	10	20
(d) Prior Inactive Service	14	05	28
(e) Total Service for Pay (c + d)	35	04	18
(f) Foreign and/or Sea Service This Period	00	00	00

- Indochina or Korea Service Since August 5, 1964: [X] Yes — No 690611-700205
- Days Accrued Leave Paid: 0
- Servicemen's Group Life Insurance Coverage: [X] $20,000
- Disability Severance Pay: NA
- Personnel Security Investigation Type: NAC/SECRET — Date Completed: 670823

Decorations, Medals, Badges, Commendations, Citations and Campaign Ribbons Awarded or Authorized:
COM(Japan)/AM/WWIIVM/NDSM/AFRESM/AFLSA w/26H OC/NESM/GCDML/VSM/w1-20S Bar/AM w/1-130LC/ PC/BSM/AFEM w/2d 10 Yr Dev/ARCAM/ARCOM

Remarks:
LAST OVERSEAS SVC:
REQUEST A COPY OF MY DD Form 214
LIST: AFFS PrimAdvFltSch/Flight School/9mos/43, RandolphFldTS/CentInstrSch/1mo/44, BryanTX/InstrumentInstr/6wks/44, FosterFldTX/P-40TrnsGNR/1mo/44, Ft WorthTX/B24 Acft Cdr/3mos/45, RoswellNM/B29 AcftCmdr/1mo/45, KeioSchCmd KeioUniv/Radar Maint/18wks/49, OA/FireConSysSch/7mos/51, Grand Rapids MI/L5AutoFltMaint/1mo/51, Williams AFB AZ/ F80 Trans/1mo/51, Nellis AFB NV/F86 Trans/1mo/51, Tyndall AFB FL/F86D Trans/2mos/52, Cincinnati OH/B47 EngMaintSch/1mo/52, Tyndall AFB FL/RadarIntcpOffSch/4mo/52, Lowrey AFB CO/DisConOffCrse/6wks/60, Air U-Maxwell Fld AL/Nuclear Wpns/6wks/60, USAAVNS/ QC 68-3 (NG)/8wks/67.

Mailing Address After Separation: 6445 Lake Sunrise Dr, Apollo Beach, FL 33570

Name, Grade and Title of Authorizing Officer: P. GORETH, CPT, FC, Asst AG

FORM 214

JAMES F. TAYLOR, JR.
CLERK CIRCUIT COURT
RECORDING DEPT.
HILLSBOROUGH CO.
TAMPA, FL 33601

Conspiracy Facts

The Vietnam Veteran in this report is Ben R. Games, PhD, Major, CW4, TCNA-6, US Army (Ret), and Major USAF (Ret). Enlisted in the Army Reserves 13 August 1942 and was retired from the Army on 11 February 1987. He served on active duty in the USAF as a Major, in the US Army on active duty as a Captain and as a CW-4. He also served in the IN Air National Guard as a Major, and in the MI Army National Guard as a CW-4. He obtained USAF Senior Pilot wings and US Army Senior Aviator Wings. The US Army retired the veteran with 70% longevity pay, 60% Combat Disability Pay, and 100% VA compensation.

> Ref; to military document, USAF order AFR 45-41 par 13d, dtd 7 Feb 1968, and US Army personnel order AR 135-215 dtd 15 Sept. 1969.

The Veteran's wife, Helen M. Games, MBA, has made their home in Okinawa, Japan, France, Vietnam,

Thailand, and the Turks & Caicos Islands. She was the 86th woman in the world to fly a helicopter and is a single/multi-engine pilot. During WWII, she sometimes flew as his copilot in a B-25 bomber. Once, during the Koran War, she flew as his RO in an F-82G night fighter, and during the Vietnam War in UH-1 and CH-47 Chinook helicopters. Visas were provided by the countries they lived in and by the US State Department. In Vietnam, they lived in a 26' trailer on a Thai Firebase called Bear Cat.

Ref; Newspaper stories, pictures, and manuscripts.

USAF Hospital at Phouc Vinh. The USAF doctors told him if they could inflate the lung he would not have to be admitted and could return to his unit. He agreed and two orderlies weighing 200 lbs. each came in to help the doctor. They held him down while the doctor inserted a tube through his nose and down into the lung to drain out the blood. It worked, and with two band-aids over the small holes, he walked to the radio control tower and hitched a ride home in a Slick helicopter in time to have supper with Helen in their trailer on Bear Cat.

In another firefight at LZ Vivian, he fell from 800 feet in his burning helicopter. This time, the wounds were more serious and included a ruptured spleen, broken ribs, and damaged hips. Once again, Ben used the USAF doctors, as they didn't even ask if he was a pilot.

No one ever asked or even suggested that he might be a combat pilot, and he was cleared for flight duty by the Bear Cat Flight Surgeon the following day. When he was operated on, Helen visited every day. After two weeks, the surgeon told him that he was being taken off all pain medicine as he was becoming addicted.

They moved him into a privet room with two beds next to the intensive care. The beds were ten feet apart. Helen was moved into the room and the surgeon told them that under no circumstances could she move the beds closer together, nor could she sleep in his bed. Then the doctor told the nurse that when lights were out at 2200 hours the door could be closed and his IV stopped until 2400 hours. The doctor told them that if he got into her bed it was okay, but he had to be connected to the IV by midnight.

Three days later while Helen was in the reading room, the Commanding Officer visited and told Ben that they had thought he wasn't going to make it but he was now free to leave when he wanted. The nurse came in after Helen returned and said there were no check-out or forms to sign. Helen was to change bandages as needed.

Ref; VA Medical report on injuries and VA Claim page 53, JO/03/06, St. Petersburg Regional Office, Par 2, sub par 5, Combat Pictures.

This report only covers the Vietnam War from 1962 to 1973, and the veteran's military active service during this period. The veteran was assigned as a USAF Nuclear Disaster Control Officer on Chanbley AB, France (1961/62), Special Investigating Officer USAF (1966), advisor Thai Marine Police (1967), Bangkok, Thailand, Camp Tien Sha, Da Nang, Vietnam (1967), and the MI Army National Guard, Detroit Riots (1967). Helicopter Aviator Training, Ft. Rucker, AL (1968). These periods are not part of this text and may show up as blank spaces in any VA files.

Ref: to military AR Form 345-170 # 103633, DD Form 256 AF, DD214s, DDForm 759, and DDAF Form 5, and VA Letters.

For the purposes of testing the Veterans Administration computer system records it should be noted that the veteran was hospitalized for injuries from an explosion of a roadside bomb that destroyed his jeep. This was during the takeover of a Japanese suicide pilot training base at Fujigaya Air Field in Japan (1946). The veteran was hospitalized in the 49th Army General Hospital because of this attack, and again when he received too much radiation during a survey of Hiroshima after the Japanese surrender. He was medi-vac'd to the United States on the US Hospital ship USS Hope in 1947. The veteran is a trained nuclear weapons officer.

Ref; medical records on file with B.C. Gibbard, VA Service Center Manager, St. Petersburg Region, copies of DD214s and orders for medical evacuation.

The Veteran was assigned as an Aircraft Commander and Instrument Instructor in a CH-47 helicopter for "B" Company, 228 Av Bn, at Bear Cat, Vietnam and to "E" Bt 82nd Artillery, 1st Cavalry Division, Vietnam on the 11 June 1969. Special combat missions came directly from Saigon Special Operations and were in support of the secret CIA Dai Phong Program supervised by Agent Gilbert H. Moriggia, pseudonym for Joseph B. Kelly.

Ref; DD Form 759 Army Flight Record, nonfiction Historical account, and biography of Joseph B. Kelly titled the "Confession of a CIA Interrogator".

On the 7 November 1969, the Army Flight Surgeon ordered CWO Ben R. Games to DNIF (duty not involving flying). The reason for the order was that he had flown over 130 hours of combat during the past thirty (30) days. His mission on the 8th November 1969 was to certify a pilot who had been in the company for six (6) months as an Aircraft Commander. The helicopter was ambushed by North Vietnamese Army soldiers and shot down in a firefight at LZ Vivian.

Ref; after action report, after action combat photos, statements from CIA

Intelligence Officer and Police Advisor of Kien Hoa Province. On the 9 November 1969 his wife, Helen, sent CWO Games to Phuoc Vinh to have his injuries looked at by the 1st Cavalry Division Flight Surgeon. The doctor determined he was bleeding internally. He was also told that there were other ruptures and a cracked rib, but these were not serious and could be repaired in the states. He was advised that the pain in his hips and chest were internal bruises from the crash of the helicopter and should disappear.

> *Ref; DD 759, Flight physical prior to combat no injuries reported (9 June 69). The Flight physical on 10 April 1970 noted combat injuries. Flight Clearance upon return to 21 noted pain in the chest from combat injuries.*

On the 13th November 1969 at Bear Cat, Vietnam, CWO Ben R. Games was awarded the Distinguished Flying Cross for heroism, General Order #718, 1st Cavalry Division for his actions in a firefight with the enemy at LZ Vivian. He was also awarded 13 Air Medals, and later the Bronze Star for action against the enemy not involving flying by "E" Bt 82nd Artillery.

> *Ref; Copies of awards, DD214, DDForm 759.*

Three times during the officer's military service he was removed from flight orders while recovering from injuries. He and his wife were taken by medi-vac or returned to the United States twice, once by the hospital ship US Hope (1947) and another time by air (1970).

After the Korean War, the veteran asked to be treated by USAF doctors or by Veterans Administration doctors. This was not done because the USAF and VA doctors were better but because they did not think of Army Warrant Officer Aviators as combat pilots.

Prior to any medical procedures, Army B/G Phillips accompanied him and spoke to the doctors. They both wore civilian clothing, and CWO Games addressed the General as "Sir" while the General addressed him as "Mr. Games." The USAF doctors may have never known that CWO Games was a combat aviator.

> Ref; copy of Army Air Corps, and USAF Personal Orders return to flight Status. USAF Surgeon Jose L. Borrero, Major, MD.

The firefight in Vietnam where his CH-47 helicopter was shot down in flames and crashed caused CWO Games to hit the cyclic with his chest so hard it cracked a rib, ruptured his spleen and stomach, and caused multiple other ruptures. A Hiatal Hernia was directly caused by trauma from enemy action during a firefight where the helicopter was destroyed by enemy fire. The

Arthritis was indirectly caused by the damage to the Veteran's hips and spine when the helicopter crashed.

> Ref; The USAF Surgeon was Jose L. Borrero, Maj, MD 079-36-0786, The VA medical records of the veteran for replacing the hips were marked service connected prior to the operations. Later the records were rebuilt to match the VA computer files and then destroyed. Copy of this VA report is attached. Department of Veterans Affairs, St. Petersburg Regional Office, Page 53, 10/03/2006. Sub Par 7 states a complete review shows that the veteran was shot, while stationed in Vietnam.

The purpose of this report is not to increase any claim for compensation from the Veterans Administration. When the Veteran first agreed to assist in this test it was only to check the accuracy of the VA computer. However, when it was discovered that Cyber Terrorists or persons unknown had compromised the VA computer system, the goal was changed to alert the Veterans Administration of the attack. Second, was to have the computer records corrected so the attack would fail.

A letter from the Department of Veterans Affairs Southern Area Office Director Mr. Michael Dusenbery dated 18 July 2006 stated that the VA has no record of any terrorists' or hackers' attack on the VA Computer System. He did however state that only data already in their system was protected.

Yet, up until 10/20/1999 the computer files indicated that the Veteran had served in the military from 11/23/1942 to 12/31/1977, US Army, Vietnam, Combat, "Yes," and the status was verified. If the computer was not compromised, then the VA had a traitor or saboteur entering false data into the VA computer. The VA records showed that the medical files had been rebuilt or changed to match the false computer data. VA Doctors and Hearing Officers using this false information were making honest, incorrect medical decisions.

Ref; VA letters, copy of computer files, Army Combat Photos, and after action reports.

The Veteran made a Medical Consultation appointment with VA Dr. James A. Carnahan, MD at the Ellenton VA Clinic for 10 July 2006 at the suggestion of the US Army Physical Disability Agency. It was a test to see if the VA Computer had been corrected to reflect the veteran's true data. The Veteran observed Dr. Carnahan using the VA computer just prior to the consultation. The doctor's statements and medical advise were consistent with the information that was in the VA computer files and did not match the actual medical history of the Veteran. One statement this doctor made was that all veterans (referring to those over 80 years old) had a Hiatal Hernia and arthritis. This veteran does not have a Hiatal Hernia; it had been repaired in a military hospital. He does have arthritis caused by the crash of his helicopter in a firefight with the enemy and the VA replace both hips.

Ref; copy of letter confirming Medical Consultation visit dtd 11 July 2006.

A De Nova Review conducted by a VA Decision Review Officer 10/03/2006 at Bay Pines VA Hospital found that the evidence of record shows that the Veteran was injured in a firefight against a hostile force in the Republic of Vietnam. Based upon this evidence, the veteran was rated a Combat Veteran and the provisions of 38 CFR 3.304 (d) apply.

Saigon Officer's Club 1967

Maj. Games and Helen Games, Thailand, 1967.

A Cry for Help

VA mishandles hundreds of documents

10/24/08, #1

A review finds papers improperly bound for the shredder in about two-thirds of benefits offices.

BY WILLIAM R. LEVESQUE
Times Staff Writer

A review of shredding bins at Department of Veterans Affairs benefits offices around the nation uncovered 489 documents improperly set aside for destruction, the VA confirmed on Thursday.

This includes documents in about two-thirds of the VA's 57 regional benefits offices, including eight at the busiest, Bay Pines in St. Petersburg, the closest office for Tampa Bay's 330,000 veterans.

These new numbers significantly expand the scope of what is turning into a major and embarrassing challenge for the VA.

And now VA investigators are trying to figure out if this one-time survey points to the likelihood that documents have been improperly destroyed for months or even years.

"Whatever this problem is, it didn't just start in the last two weeks," said Dave Autry, a spokesman for Disabled American Veterans. "It'd be unreasonable to assume that. Who knows what's been destroyed."

The documents, which didn't have duplicates at the VA, would have been critical in deciding veteran pension and disability claims. As a result, many veterans are asking whether their delayed or denied claims were affected by lost paperwork.

"Now that the VA's been caught with their pants down, everybody's got to wonder if they're affected."

» See VA, 9A

From the front page

10/24/08 #2

» VA continued from 1A

VA continues ban on shredding papers

said Paul Freeland, 72, a Marine veteran from Pinellas Park who accuses the VA of losing his paperwork on a denied disability claim.

With two VA attorneys convicted in the mid 1990s of purposefully destroying paperwork to ease their workload, one question the VA hopes to answer:

Is any of this deliberate?

The VA says it doesn't know.

"This is disturbing and very concerning," said Mike Walcoff, the VA's deputy undersecretary

some regional offices reported no problem documents because the paperwork was routinely destroyed before the VA's review.

It also is possible, he said, that a small portion of the 489 may ultimately prove to have been adequately processed.

Walcoff declined to say if the VA is considering reopening any denied claims in cases in which a veteran alleged that the agency had lost paperwork.

"I can't speculate," he said. "There are legal issues involved."

for benefits in Washington, D.C. "We're doing our best to get the number to zero."

The VA is continuing its unprecedented national ban of all shredding at its benefits offices until it finds a way to guarantee documents aren't being improperly destroyed.

At benefits offices in Cleveland and Columbia, S.C., two employees have been placed on administrative leave after the VA found evidence they may have deliberately placed documents in a shredding bin.

About 259 of the misplaced documents found nationally are tied to these two cities and St. Louis, the VA said.

Walcoff said the VA is reviewing how it safeguards all documents and noted that the VA review isn't necessarily confined to shredding operations.

Asked if the VA is investigating whether unprocessed documents may be languishing in desks, briefcases or at the homes of VA employees, Walcoff said, "We're looking at all possibilities."

The VA began its internal inquiry after its Inspector General — the agency's independent watchdog — found problems this month in four cities during a routine audit. The IG has not finished its report.

Those cities were St. Louis, Detroit, St. Petersburg and Waco, Texas.

Walcoff noted it is possible that

The benefits offices are among the most paper-intensive in the federal bureaucracy, processing 162-million pages a year. The VA said the current situation points to the need for a faster transition to computer records.

One of the most common complaints by veterans seeking benefits is that the VA loses documents.

That can delay by months or even years a decision on a claim and can lead to a denial.

Gordon Erspamer, a California claims attorney who has worked on litigation against the VA, said the agency has long known it had a problem with improperly destroyed paperwork.

"This has been going on for many, many years," he said. VA claims workers "are under such intense pressure to process claims quickly that they look for the easiest way to deny a claim. Instead of making a decision, it's often better to just lose a medical report."

Erspamer said VA workers have a financial incentive to process claims quickly because they essentially work on a quota system. That, he said, encourages some to "lose" paperwork.

"Tens of thousands of veterans simply die with their claims pending," he said.

William R. Levesque can be reached at levesque@sptimes.com or (813) 269-5306.

A Cry for Help

House panel will target VA shredding

Behind in the polls, Sen. John McCain has 10 days left to turn the tide his way.

Rep. C.W. Bill Young says the problem may be widespread and involve legal sanctions.

BY WILLIAM R. LEVESQUE
Times Staff Writer

A House committee overseeing the Department of Veterans Affairs will hold hearings next month to question VA leaders about documents improperly marked for shredding at agency offices around the nation.

Rep. Bob Filner, D-Calif., chairman of the House Committee on Veterans Affairs, said Friday that he was outraged by revelations that papers crucial to deciding veteran disability and pension claims were being destroyed by VA workers.

"These guys remind me of the Keystone Kops," Filner said. "This completely shatters confidence in the whole VA system. These documents are matters of life and death for some of these veterans."

Rep. C.W. Bill Young, R-Indian Shores, is not on the committee but supports having hearings and suggested the problem might be widespread.

» See VA, 7A

Oct. 25, 08 - #1

Ben R. Games, PhD

Oct. 25, 08 — #2

From the front page

» VA continued from 1A

House panel to review VA handling of papers

Some VA employees could face legal problems, he said.

Filner said he will hold the hearings the week of Nov. 17, when a lame-duck session of Congress is expected to convene to consider an economic stimulus package.

Filner said among those he will call to testify are VA Secretary James Peake and investigators for the agency's independent watchdog, the inspector general.

A VA spokeswoman declined to comment on the hearings or Filner's statements. But the VA said it expects to cooperate with any House investigation.

Filner, a frequent critic of the VA, said he wanted to know how far back this problem went and said he thought the agency needed new leadership.

"I think there are some employees at the VA who don't want to do the work," Filner said.

"And management allows this to happen."

The VA inspector general earlier this month found problems with documents improperly marked for disposal at benefits offices in four cities: St. Petersburg, Detroit, St. Louis and Waco, Texas.

While the inspector general investigation continued, the VA began a separate inquiry that found nearly 500 documents improperly placed in shredder bins in about two-thirds of the agency's 57 benefits offices.

At Bay Pines in St. Petersburg, the busiest benefits office in the nation, investigators found eight misplaced documents.

Young said he spoke with investigators for the inspector general in St. Petersburg this week. "What they tell me convinces me that it's bad," Young said. "And I think some people are probably in legal trouble."

But Young declined to release details or say if any employee of the St. Petersburg office deliberately threw away veterans' paperwork. Young said investigators asked him not to release information until their work is finished.

"I don't think they know the full scale of the problem yet," Young said. "I'm afraid this might be a widespread and long-term situation."

Alison Aikele, a VA spokeswoman in Washington, said a national ban on all shredding in benefits offices remains in effect. That ban will continue until the agency settles on a policy to guarantee key documents are not improperly destroyed.

William R. Levesque can be reached at levesque@sptimes.com or (813) 269-5306.

VA says it shred 10/23/08 papers in error

Eight documents in shredding bins may be a sign of more, the agency acknowledges.

BY WILLIAM R. LEVESQUE
Times Staff Writer

ST. PETERSBURG — Employees in the nation's busiest Department of Veterans Affairs benefits office at Bay Pines in St. Petersburg improperly placed eight documents in shredding bins, the VA said on Wednesday.

The discovery during a random, one-time survey points to a disquieting possibility that the VA acknowledges it is now investigating:

Have workers for months or even years destroyed untold numbers of documents critical in deciding if the VA owes a veteran a pension or disability payment?

"That's the obvious question," said Mike Walcoff, the VA's deputy undersecretary for benefits in Washington. "We can't answer that at this point."

The VA's 56 regional offices began investigating allegations of improperly shredded documents last week after the agency's Inspector General found problems in four cities — St. Louis, Detroit, St. Petersburg and Waco, Texas.

Of the eight documents in St. Petersburg, the VA said never would have been critical in deciding a veteran's claim. The eighth document had already been processed but should have been returned to the veteran rather than marked for shredding.

"This is not something we're comfortable with," Walcoff said. "I won't say anything to diminish the importance of the doc-

» See SHRED, 7B

VA admits mistake in shredding

uments veterans send us. We didn't take care of some of them like we should."

The St. Petersburg benefits office, covering the entire state and its 1.8-million veterans, processed 60,000 pension or disability claims last year.

As the VA and Inspector General continue their investigations, the VA is extending a national ban on all shredding in its benefits offices until working out a policy to safeguard documents.

The VA could not provide information on the findings in other benefits offices around the country. And the Inspector General — the VA's independent watchdog — isn't finished with its separate inquiry.

The VA has scheduled a morning conference call today with the representatives of the six largest veterans service groups in the nation to provide an update on the VA's investigation.

Joe Davis, spokesman for Veterans of Foreign Wars, said he is worried that findings of improperly discarded papers point to a much bigger problem.

"This could go back many years," Davis said. "It's all about attention to detail. VA employees have to remember that the signature on a claims form belongs to a real human being. It's not just a piece of paper."

So far, Walcoff said, the VA doesn't know how the documents in St. Petersburg made their way to the shredding bins or who is responsible. And neither can the VA say if the documents were dumped by accident or on purpose.

In the mid 1990s, two employees of the VA's veterans appeal board in Washington, D.C., acknowledged discarding documents to lighten their work load. Those cases first came to light on the Web site VAwatchdog.org, which broke the shredding story earlier this month.

Walcoff noted that the VA's benefits offices are among the most paper-intensive bureaucracies in the federal government, processing 162-million pages of paper throughout the nation.

And while the VA is moving increasingly to electronic records, Walcoff said, the transition is far from complete.

Speaking of improper shredding, Walcoff said, "This just screams out at us to move faster so we get to the point where we're not dealing with all that paper."

Lost or misplaced documents are one of the most common complaints by veterans, who often wait years for the VA to decide if they are owed a pension or disability payment.

But to veterans, it is usually impossible to prove that the agency has lost their paperwork. So they are often forced to simply send new copies, greatly delaying their claims.

"Until now, all we had was a veteran's statement" that something was lost, Walcoff said. "When we hear those types of comments now, we're certainly going to listen to them in a different light based on what's happened in the last couple of weeks."

Marine veteran Tony Vieria, 66, of St. Petersburg said the VA once denied his medical claim based on another veteran's record. His claim was later approved once the paperwork was straightened out.

"Everybody knows that if you send the VA any original document, you're crazy," Vieria said. "God only knows where it's going to go. You'll never see it again."

William R. Levesque can be reached at (813) 269-5306 or at levesque@sptimes.com.

A Cry for Help

CAUTION: NOT TO BE USED FOR IDENTIFICATION PURPOSES	ANY ALTERATIONS IN SHADED AREAS RENDER FORM VOII
	**CORRECTION TO DD FORM 214,** **CERTIFICATE OF RELEASE OR DISCHARGE FROM ACTIVE DUTY**

1. NAME (Last, First, Middle)	2. DEPARTMENT, COMPONENT AND BRANCH	3. SOCIAL SECURITY NUMBER (Also, Service Number if applicable)
GAMES, BEN ROBERT	ARMY-ARNG MI	༝⸺ 1165
4. MAILING ADDRESS (Include ZIP Code) 6445 LAKE SUNRISE DRIVE APOLLO BEACH, FLORIDA 33570		

5. ORIGINAL DD FORM 214 IS CORRECTED AS INDICATED BELOW:

ITEM NO.	CORRECTED TO READ
	SEPARATION DATE ON DD FORM 214 BEING CORRECTED: 77 12 31
26	ADD: NATIONAL DEFENSE SERVICE MEDAL//VIETNAM SERVICE MEDAL W/2 BRONZE SERVICE STARS//REPUBLIC OF VIETNAM GALLANTRY CROSS W/PALM UNIT CITATION BADGE //REPUBLIC OF VIETNAM CIVIL ACTIONS HONOR MEDAL, FIRST CLASS UNIT CITATION BADGE//REPUBLIC OF VIETNAM CAMPAIGN MEDAL W/DEVICE(1960)//NOTHING FOLLOWS

6. DATE (YYYYMMDD)	7. OFFICIAL AUTHORIZED TO SIGN			
	a. TYPED NAME (Last, First, Middle Initial)	b. GRADE	c. TITLE	d. SIGNATURE
20080514	SANDERS, SALLY A.	GS-09	SUPV HR SPC (MIL) ARBA-STL	*Sally A. Sanders*

DD FORM 215, FEB 2000   PREVIOUS EDITION IS OBSOLETE.   MEMBER - 1

Helen arriving at the Saigon Airport.

PROLOGUE

Chief of the Military Awards Branch, Lt/Colonel Sylvia A. Bennett, has written that Purple Heart criteria requires that it only be awarded to soldiers for wounds and injuries received as a result of enemy action. The wounds must have required treatment by medical personnel and have been made a matter of official record. Also, official documentation reflecting medical treatment for the wound or injuries must be provided.

The letter also stated that a Purple Heart medal could not be granted to the men and women wounded by enemy action unless they were on the Vietnam Historical Casualty List. The author could not verify the Army Order that created two lists for soldiers wounded or killed by enemy actions.

On 25 April 1962, President John F. Kennedy, by executive order, extended the award of the Purple Heart to all military and civilian nationals of the United

States wounded while serving under competent authority with the armed forces of the United States. His order also stated that it included *all who have or who may hereafter be wounded or killed.* President Ronald Reagan amended the order on 23 February 1984 to include those wounded or killed as a result of an terrorist attack.

The Executive Orders of two Presidents did not authorize any branch of military service to place restrictions on, or to authorize changes to, the executive orders. The author's combat injuries happened when his helicopter was shot down by enemy fire at LZ Vivian. The author was awarded the Distinguished Flying Cross but not the Purple Heart for his participation in this firefight, as he was not on the Military Awards Branch Vietnamese Historical Casualty List.

This is the conspiracy to change history by misleading American Citizens. The US Army Human Resources Command, Awards and Decorations Branch, is in Fort Knox, KY. The Chief of the Awards and Decoration Branch was Lt/Colonel Stewart L. Stephenson, Jr., US Army, in October 2010. The letter to Dr. Ben R. Games, PhD was an answer to his request for President Barack H. Obama to approve adding the Vietnam Wound Medal to the DD Form 215, Feb. 2000, Date: 20080514, Official: Saunders, Sally A., Grade GS-09, Title: SUPV

SPC HR (MIL ARBA-STL). The Original DD Form 214 was corrected to read: ITEM 26, ADD: National Defense Service Vietnam Service Medal W/2 Bronze Service Stars, Republic of Vietnam Gallantry Cross W/ Palm, Unit Citation Badge, Republic of Vietnam Civil Actions Honor Medial, First Class Unit Citation Badge, Republic of Vietnam Campaign W/Device (1960).

The author learned later that none of the soldiers in the body bags that were delivered to the Saigon Mortuary Pad from the firefight at LZ Vivien on the 8th November 1969 received a Purple Heart. The mission was secret, and the soldiers were individual volunteers. The enemy or someone against the Vietnam War was conspiring with the North Vietnamese to fool the American people. Today, the battle for controlling the minds and souls of the American people is still the ultimate goal of these conspirators.

While the author is a disabled Combat Veteran of the 1st Cavalry Division, holder of the Distinguished Flying Cross, and can no longer toe the line for military assignments, he has been trying to help the Veterans Administration recognize the men and woman who fought for our country. In his research for the Modern World History stories, he writes about how he found two soldiers who would not surrender when the enemy attacked. They, too, were declared by the Military

Awards Branch not to be Historic Casualties. The author believes that there may be many more veterans and civilians not on the correct list.

David Lee Walker, SP5, 25th Infantry Division was injured by falling from a UH-1 Army Helicopter that was shot down while inserting his Infantry Squad into a hot LZ on Thanksgiving day 1967. He received medical aid for his back and pelvic injuries, while providing covering fire to allow other soldiers to reinforce his team. All members of his squad were injured or killed in the firefight. The Army Medic who was putting a bandage on the man next to the Sergeant must have forgotten to give him a medical receipt for his wounds.

There were 150 soldiers of the 25th Infantry Division that were sent to Vietnam with Sergeant Walker. At the end of 363 days of combat, 27 men were left. The others were killed or wounded so badly they had been returned Stateside. Some may have made the Historic Casualty List and others may not have.

The second time Sergeant Walker was wounded by enemy fire occurred while on a patrol in the Michelin Rubber Plantation. A sniper's gunshot from behind penetrated his backpack. The wounds did not stop him from supporting his squad in the firefight. He was treated by an on-site medic while continuing to fire his M-16.

Sergeant Walker was wounded a third time while defending his Company Command Bunker. An enemy RPG round knocked him off the top of the command bunker and he hit the ground 100 feet away. His BAR was destroyed, and he had other injures that kept him on the ground. An Army Medic crawled over and gave him pain killers and another M-16. This action took place on 1 January 1968, Tay Ninh Province, Vietnam.

Sergeant Walker was awarded a Bronze Star with a "V" device. He was not considered a Historical Casualty, possibility because he would not stop fighting the enemy. In fact, he was given company punishment for refusing to leave by medi-vac helicopter until the firefight was over. Punishment was having to make a body count of the dead enemy soldiers.

During research for the nonfiction book *Confession of a CIA Interrogator*, the author learned that **Mr. Joseph B. Kelly, USAF**, 20 year veteran and CIA Contract Agent was working for the US Department of Labor and Army as a South Vietnam police advisor. He was staying in the American Embassy at Ben Tre, Vietnam, when the North Vietnamese attacked. He was wounded when a mortar round hit the roof over his head. The author personally interviewed **Colonel Geoffrey T. Baker,** (now retired infantry) who lead the counter attack and later received the Bronze Star for heroism.

Mr. Kelly, while wounded from enemy fire, protected Maj/General Timmes and organized the defense of the American Embassy. After successfully repelling the enemy forces, Mr. Kelly was treated for his wounds at the MACV Hospital. The attack on the Embassy and its defense was classified secret by the US State Department.

A letter from the Department of the Army, Deputy Chief of Staff G-4, 2461 Eisenhower Avenue, Alexandria, VA stated that no Army Commander or State Department Manger had authorized Mr. Kelly to conduct a defense of the US Embassy during this firefight, therefore he did not meet the criteria for the Purple Heart. The firefight and medical reports were classified secret.

The author is now over 87 years old and is presently reviewing the letters written and received over the years concerning the request for the award of a Purple Heart for Mr. Kelly and Sergeant Walker. It was pointed out to him by the Director of the VFW that the Commanders of the Army Awards Branch might not have personally read the letters because they were forwarded to them by President Bush and President Obama. The answers to the letters were actually signed by someone other than the Department Commander in the Army Awards Branch who could also be a supporter of the "Conspiracy To Change History."

Copies of the letters and pictures contained in this report were used to allow researchers of history to seek the truth. Each individual must judge for him or herself if this is truly a conspiracy to aid the enemy in its efforts to destroy our nation or just simply incompetence. This report is copyrighted and may be used or copied by students or researchers for their work. To obtain a release or permission to use these documents, all a researcher needs to do is to purchase a copy of this report from Fideli Publishing, Inc. Keep it with your file on releases for documents and pictures. The publisher will keep a list of individuals who have received a release to use these documents and pictures. Do not send claims or documents to the publisher. All requests for assistance should be sent to your Congressional Representative.

Remember, it was the Conspirators who convinced the author to request the Army Board for Correction of Military Records, 1901 South Bell Street 2nd Floor, Arlington, VA 22202-4508. The records had already been changed by a Cyber Terrorist attack on the VA computers. Hackers had removed or changed all the VA medical information verifying the author's service in Vietnam. The Army Board for Correction of Military Records were correct, because they were ruling on a corrupt file. Maybe the Conspirators already knew that other hackers had changed many veterans' medical records in the VA Computers.

This Historical Text is an attempt by the author to honor those men and women who worked in the shadows to help keep America free, and to the families of Vietnamese War Veterans who were not on the Historical Casualty List.

Ben and Helen on Waikiki Beach, Hawaii. They were evacuated on the hospital ship USS Hope after Ben's first assignment in the far east.

Ben R. Games, PhD

The Purple Heart
Then and Now

Attached to the piece of dark blue cloth is a purple heart of silk, bound with braid and edged with lace. The cloth is believed to be part of the uniform tunic of a soldier of the Continental Army.

There is no name, rank or regimental insignia on the piece of cloth. The Purple Heart is displayed in Washington, D.C., at the Society of the Cincinnati's Anderson House Museum and another at the New Windsor Cantonment site at New Windsor, NY. The Purple Heart itself is what signified a hero in the Revolutionary War.

The Purple Heart was awarded to three soldiers - Sgts. Elijah Churchill, William Brown, and Daniel Bissell, Jr. On May 3, 1783, Churchill and Brown received the Purple Heart, then called the Badge of Military Merit, from Gen. George Washington, its designer and creator. Bissell received his on June 10, 1783. These three were the only recipients of the award during the Revolutionary War.

On August 7, 1782, at his Newburg, NY headquarters, Washington devised two badges of distinction to be worn by enlisted men and noncommissioned officers. The first was a chevron to be worn on the left sleeve of the coat. It signified loyal military service. Three years of service with "bravery, fidelity, and good conduct" were the criteria for earning this badge; two chevrons meant six years of service.

The second, named the Badge of Military Merit, was the "figure of a heart in purple cloth or silk-edged with narrow lace or binding". This badge was for "any singularly meritorious action" and permitted the wearer to pass guards and sentinels without challenge. The honoree's name and regiment were inscribed in a Book of Merit.

After the Revolutionary War, no more American soldiers received the Badge of Military Merit. It was not until October 10, 1927, that Army Chief of Staff, General Charles P. Summerall, directed a draft bill be sent to Congress "to revive the Badge of Military Merit."

The Army withdrew the bill on January 3, 1928, but the Office of the Adjutant General filed all correspondence for possible future use.

Although a number of private efforts were made to have the medal reinstituted, it wasn't until January 7,m 1931, that Summerall's successor, General Douglas MacArthur, confidentially reopened the case. His object was to have a new medal issued on the bicentennial of George Washington's birth.

Miss Elizabeth Will, in the Office of the Quartermaster General, created the design from guidelines provided her. The only difference in her design is that a sprig appeared where the profile of Washington is on the present Purple Heart.

John R. Sinnock of the Philadelphia Mint made the plaster model in May 1931. The War Department announced the new award on February 22, 1932.

After the award was reinstated, recipients of a Meritorious Service Citation Certificate during World War I, along with other eligible soldiers, could exchange their award for the Purple Heart.

At the same time, revisions to Army regulations defined the conditions of the award: *"A wound which necessitates treatment by a medical officer and which is received in action with an enemy, may in the judgment of the commander authorized to make the award, be construed as resulting from a singularly meritorious act of essential service."*

At that time the Navy Department did not authorize the issue of the Purple Heart, but Franklin D. Roosevelt amended that by Executive Order on December 3, 1942, with the Coast Guard beginning December 6, 1941.

President Harry S. Truman retroactively extended eligibility to the Navy, Marine Corps, and Coast Guard to April 3, 1917, to cover World War I.

President John F. Kennedy extended eligibility on April 25, 1962, to "any civilian national of the United States who, while serving under competent authority in any capacity with an armed force ..., has been, or may hereafter be, wounded."

President Ronald Reagan, on February 23, 1984, amended President Kennedy's order, to include those wounded or killed as a result of "an international terrorist attack."

Army regulations, amended June 20, 1969, state that any "member of the Army who was awarded the Purple Heart for meritorious achievement or service, as opposed to wounds received in action between December 7, 1941, and September 22, 1943, may apply for award of an appropriate decoration in lieu of the Purple Heart."

There are no records of the first individual who received the revived and redesigned Purple Heart. Local posts of the American Legion and the Adjutant Generals of State National Guards both held ceremonies to honor recipients.

What Washington wrote in his Orderly book on August 7, 1782, still stands today: *"The road to glory in a patriot army and a free country is thus open to all. This order is also to have retrospect to the earliest stages of the war, and to be considered as a permanent one."*

Shortly after the award was reinstituted, a group of combat wounded veterans in Ansonia, CT, formed the first chapter of the civilian organization whose membership was composed of recipients of the decoration. Their action gave birth to a fraternal body which, until then, had been but a record on paper. The living organization grew rapidly during and after World War II and is now a nationwide body of men. It became known as the "Military Order of the Purple Heart of the United States of America, Inc." (M.O.P.H.). The organization was chartered by Congress by H.R. 13558, which became Public Law 85-761, on August 26, 1958.

The M.O.P.H. maintains its national headquarters in Springfield, VA, and has chapters throughout the United States. The organization represents veterans' interests before Congress, the Veterans Administration, the Department of Defense, and elsewhere.

In addition, the Order is proud of its key role in the National Service Program. The Order maintains a full time National Service Director who supervises the over 300 salaried and volunteer service officers. All Purple Heart Service Officers have been accredited by the Veterans Administration. They provide assistance and representation for all veterans, their dependents and survivors, in obtaining their rightful entitlements and benefits. All services are FREE.

For additional information on how to join, write or call:

Military Order of the Purple Heart
5413-B Backlick Road
Springfield, VA 22151
(703) 642-5360

South Korean Embassy officers and Ben, Vietnam.

HISTORICAL DOCUMENTS

These documents and pictures were used by the author to help verify the historical facts of this TEXTBOOK. This is a nonfiction record of the combat injuries of Major Ben R. Games, PhD, Joseph B. Kelly, CIA Contract Agent, USAF Retired, and David Lee Walker, SP5, 25 Infantry Division during the Vietnam War.

Those individuals who have personal knowledge of the events described herein or who would like to learn more about Ben and Helen's adventures may contact Fideli Publishing Inc.

This report was written to record that someone in the Military Awards Branch was actually trying to change history by keeping two casualty lists for the Vietnam War. Only veterans on the approved list were issued a Purple Heart.

Fideli Publishing, Inc
119 W. Morgan St.
Martinsville, IN 46151

Phone: 1-888-343-3542
www.FideliPublishing.com

The author is a retired Life Member of the USAF Association and Distinguished Flying Cross Society. He is also a member of the North American Aviation "Mach Buster's Club" in the F-86 Sabre Jet. Some copies of the author's flight records are included to help the reader understand the Air Force Form 5 (rev. Oct. 1945) plus the US Army DD Form 759.

CH-34 Helicopters - Saigon 1967

A Cry for Help

U.S. Army Servival School Ft. Rucker, AL. Helen on the right. Taken prior to leaving for Vietnam 1969

Ben R. Games, PhD

TO WHOM IT MY CONCERN.

Ref: Request by Joseph B. Kelly, CIA Contract Agent, (ret), 808 Allison Dr, Jonesborough, TN 37659 to verify his actions during the Vietnam War.

I am the author of a book named "Confessions of a CIA Interrogator". It was written about Joseph B. Kelly who used the CIA pseudonym of Gilbert H. Moriggia in Vietnam and his own name while working as a police advisor assigned to the US Army; paid by the US Department of Labor as a GS-13. The story is nonfiction and a true account of Joe Kelly's actions

I worked for the Saigon Combat Operations Center and was supported by the Korean Military Attaché, the South Vietnamese Minister of Information Mr. Cat Lee, 1st Cavalry Division "E" Bt 82nd Artillery, and "B" Company of the 228 Bn. My wife Helen and I lived on a Thi Firebase named Bearcat (1969).

When I wrote about Joe time was compressed so the story would not have long periods where nothing was going on. I've found that time speeds up in a firefight and lasts forever when you are sitting in the dark slapping mosquitoes waiting for daylight.

All the firefights and combat action that Joe was in where I wasn't directly involved were not include in the book until I had personally interviewed all parties involved. On two occasions were he was wounded in direct contact with the enemy I reviewed and made a report to the Saigon Combat Operations Center. The medical reports were classified Secret by the State Department; including the doctors medical treatment.

I also changed the exact location of some incidences that may still be classified. Actually I tried not to use or name anyone in the story who was a traitor to the United States as this was about the heroism of patriots who work in the shadows.

Dr. Ben R. Games, PhD
814 Church St # 102
Ellenton, FL 34222

A Cry for Help

Helen Flying a OH-6, "E" Battery Helicopter.

Helen and son Jon (age 16) helping to move orphans from the combat zone.

Ben and son Jon.

Christmas 1969 in Vietnam.

A Cry for Help

Helen Games in Saigon, Vietnam 1967.

Ben and Helen's home Bear Cat, Vietnam. Patching up after a rocket attack — 160 holes

Chaplain Funches with Ben and Helen Games by chapel.

Ben R. Games, PhD

Flying over the Da Nang River 1967

68

A VFW BIOGRAPHY
by Vickie Lopez

With writings of VFW Life Member
BEN R. GAMES, PhD

Ben R. Games, PhD, Major, CW4, TCNA-6, flew bombers and night fighters during World War II. Then jet fighters during the Korean War period and Chinook helicopters in Vietnam for the 1st Cavalry Division. He is a life member of the North American Mach Busters Club and the Distinguished Flying Cross Society with 737 recorded combat hours. He is also a life member of Army Aviation Class 43K, 1st Cavalry Division Association, MOAA, USAF Association, VHPA, National Guard Association of the United States, Camp Graying Officers Club, the Veterans of Foreign Wars, the American Legion, and the DAV. After 35 years, he retired from military flying and in 1980 became the General Manager of the Turks and Caicos National Airlines.

During his military service, Ben was awarded the Distinguished Flying Cross, Bronze Star, 13 Air Medals, Army Commendation Medal with "V" device, National Defense Service Medal w/3 Bronze Service Stars, MI Medal of Valor w/Oak leaf cluster, Legion of Merit with Oak Leaf cluster, Vietnam Campaign Medal w/1960 Device, Republic of Vietnam Gallantry Cross w/Palm Unit Citation, Republic of Vietnam Civil Actions Medal of Honor Medal, and Senate Life Gold Medial.

His Story Reads Like An Adventure Novel

Gentle Ben believes that if you want to see into the future you must study history. Politicians sometimes try to change history by rewriting it. They know that history is a window looking into the future. If you look into a telescope at a star you are looking into the past. To know what a star did in the past will give you a good guess at what it may do in the future. He has concluded that it is the same with people and governments.

Ben has written many books. Most are nonfiction but some are based on conjecture. He starts many of his stories with a chapter on his life as a young man or about one of his life experiences. Ben is a family man who believes that everyone has a story to tell. He tells everyone who will listen that these stories and poems will enrich the family's history. To help make it happen he started placing family stories, and poems in book form under the name "Little Big BOOKS ©" Each Games Clan member's work has his or her name and bio is listed with their writings submitted for publication.

From These Writings We Glean His Truth

Ben Robert Games was born May 5, 1924 in Elkhart, Indiana to Robert B. (Bob) and Betty Jo Games. As a child, he was called Benny Bob. During 1930 through 1937, Benny Bob lived with his parents in the western United States during the building of Hover Dam and Boulder City, Nevada. It was during the Great Depression, and people died from hunger during this period. Finding food for the family was the main job of the men and boys. His father worked at many jobs ranging from bootlegger, prospector, miner and blacksmith.

Benny Bob was ten years old when his father worked running a pack train of burros for the U.S. Geological Survey Teams during the building of Hover Dam. It took all day to drive from Las Vegas, Nevada to the Colorado River watering point and base camp. There was a wooden platform built fifty feet back from the river's edge. On the platform were ten 50-gallon wooden barrels with the tops cut out. The barrels were filled with river water that was full of mud and silt. When the mud had settled to the bottom of the barrels the clean water was drawn out, and then poured into five-gallon canvas water bags. The outsides of the bags were kept wet until the pack train started out. This kept the water cool. Four water bags were placed on each pack animal with the other supplies tied on top of the packsaddle. Each survey team was made up of three to five men and each pack train had at least ten burros in it. The plan was for each man to have ten gallons of water per day; with a delivery of food and water made every other day.

As the survey teams moved further from the watering point, the longer it took to make the trip. Because of the high canyon walls and the lack of places to get water, the pack train grew to twenty burros. To control the burros the father walked leading the way. Following the pack animals, the mother and son rode their burros. Benny Bob's burro carried a rolled up blanket, then-two jackets, and a bag of jerky on its packsaddle. Around his waist were a small cloth-covered metal canteen and a small bullwhip. The end of the whip was split with three leather knotted tips. Benny Bob could hit a rattlesnake or scorpion with that tip and kill them every time. He wore a hat, shorts, heavy walking shoes, and sometimes a shirt. His mother's burro carried her, two one-gallon canvas water bags, and a small cloth covered canteen. She wore a light dress with a large brimmed hat. As they had no saddles they couldn't carry their walking sticks. They were one day out of base camp and another day from Las Vegas. If a rattlesnake bit someone there was no way to get help even if they could make it back to camp as the survey crew had to have water to live.

Benny Bob's burro, Jack, was the one-year-old son of the burro his mother rode. It had never been weaned, and it never let its mother get out of sight. As they rode through the canyons and over the mountain trails Jack would stop to nibble a bit of cactus, weed or dried grass. Benny Bob tried to make his burro catch up to the pack train and its mother by kicking, hitting or even using the whip, but he couldn't make it move. However, just as soon as its mother's tail started to disappear around a bend or rock Jack went from full stop to a run until his muzzle could touch her. Jack only had two speeds: stop or full speed ahead. Sometimes the trail was so narrow and the cliffs so high it didn't seem as if Jack could make the turns at full speed but he never missed a step. When he couldn't find anything else to nibble on the little burro would turn and bite his rider. Benny Bob spent his days hanging on, trying to keep from being eaten by the burro, and daydreaming.

When near the surveyor's camp they would find a large boulder to rest on while waiting for his father and the pack train to return. Why a large rock instead of shade from the desert sun? Snakes like shade and avoid the sun during the heat of the day. Sometimes mountain sheep would pass near the boulder as they went on up into the mountains looking for food. His mother's burro was always hobbled, and when the wild horses came by it was even tied. Jack was never tied as he wouldn't leave his mother. The water canteen and his packsaddle with the supplies were taken off while they waited for the his father to return. From one to three hours would go by before the trip home began.

As the surveying camps got further from the river it took longer to make the round trip. His father had to leave every day with a pack train to keep two survey gangs working. He would start at daylight and wouldn't get back until after dark. On these trips Benny Bob and his mother would stay in camp, fill the barrels with river water, and get the packs ready for the next day's water delivery.

On one particular trip his father was tired and had hung his canteen with the pistol on a burro's packsaddle. He usually made everyone carry his or her own canteen and weapons but this trip was different. The pack train was following the lead burro and his father was walking along following them as they headed towards home. It was the hottest part of the day, around 1500 hours when his father needed a drink of water. He reached for the canteen, and the burro trotted ahead keeping out of reach. This went on for over an hour with the burro staying just ahead of his grasping fingers.

They were soon coming to a place on the trail where one burro couldn't pass another. His father knew when they got to that point the burro couldn't run ahead, and he could catch up. His father walked along planning what would happen to that burro when he got his pistol. They finally arrived at the narrow part of the trail, and his father ran forward trying to catch hold of the packsaddle. The burro just nipped the burro ahead him which made all the other burros start to run. He still couldn't get within three feet of the water canteen and his pistol. His father soon realized that there was no way to get the canteen. He found a big rock that gave some shade where he could rest and wait for the desert to cool. Any rattlesnake around would just have to take its chances. His father had to have protection from the hot sun so he stopped, and all the burros stopped with him. He waited for sundown and the desert to cool as there was not going to be any more stops on the way back to camp. As soon as the sun disappeared his father started down the trail with the water carrying burro staying just out of reach. He never got closer than an arms reach of the canteen. It was 2300 hours and his father had been on the desert trail for over 10 hours without water.

Benny Bob and his mother heard him as he arrived in camp. His father fell headfirst into one of the barrels of drinking water; tipping the barrel over as he splashed water all over himself. He still hadn't spoken to anyone, but when he could stand up, he reached for Benny Bob's rifle, and without one word shot the burro dead. Then he walked over to its backpack, took the canteen it was carrying, and started to drink.

These experiences taught Benny Bob lessons that he used for his entire military career. Never fight unless it was to win, and never hit someone with your fist if a club was handy. Never leave a live enemy behind you, and never trust a jackass to help in case of trouble. The most important lesson of all was to carry your own canteen.

In 1935 when Mussolini invaded Ethiopia Haile Selassie issued this mobilization order. "Everyone will be mobilized, and all boys old enough to carry a spear will be sent to Addis Ababa. Married men will take their wives to carry food and to cook. Those without wives will take any woman without a husband. Women with small babies need not come. The blind and those who cannot walk, or any reason cannot carry a spear, are exempt. Anyone found at home after receipt of this order will be hanged." While this order cannot be found in the US Army rule book Ben still believed it was a good order and took, Helen, his wife with him.

Ben's military duties and responsibilities allowed him to live in different countries around the globe which included Japan, France, Vietnam, Okinawa, and Grand Turk. Along with Helen (Whirly Girl #86, the eighty-sixth woman in the world to become a helicopter pilot), they made their home in all of these lands.

Helen M. Amsden, the girl from Goshen, Indiana met and married Ben R. Games, the man from Elkhart, Indiana on the 5th of June 1943 in Fort Stockton, Texas, and again at the Mormon Temple in Salt Lake City, Utah on March 25, 1959. Just to be sure that she knew what the man from Elkhart was doing, she became a single engine and multi-engine pilot. Then when he became a test pilot, who sometimes landed without an engine, she earned a glider pilot rating. Helen has flown as his copilot during WWII in Army BT-13, C-45 and B-25 aircraft. Once in Okinawa she flew as an RO (radar operator) in his F-82G night fighter. In Vietnam she traveled in his Chinook CH-47 helicopter "City of Elkhart." Ben and Helen have two sons and three grandchildren.

RICHES
by Helen M. Games, MBA

The more you give
the more you get.
The more you laugh,
the less you fret.
The more you do unselfishly,
the more you live abundantly.
The more of everything you share,
the more you always
have to spare.
The more you love,
the more you'll find.
That life is good,
and friends are kind.
For only what we give away,
enriches us from day to day.

A Cry for Help

Bear Cat Vietnam, 1969.

Bear Cat Vietnam, 1969.

A Cry for Help

Bear Cat Vietnam, 1969.

Fashion show, Officer's Club, Vietnam, 1969.

A Cry for Help

CIA Contact Agent police advisor for US Army — Joe, 1969.

The Army cemetery, Thailand, 1967.

Bear Cat, Vietnam, 1969.

A Cry for Help

TRANSLATION 26 June 1970

Vietnamese Citation for award of Bronze Star to English

for Joseph B. Kelly (1970)

```
                                                REPUBLIC OF VIETNAM
                                                KIEN HOA PROVINCE
                                                PHUNG HOANG COMMITTEE
                                                PERMANENT CENTER
```

TO: LT COLONEL PROVINCE CHIEF
CONCURRENTLY KIEN HOA SECTOR COMMANDER

SUBJECT: Propose a official award for an American Advisor and his assistant

Dear Sir,

I respectfully report to you that:

1- Mr Joseph B. Kelly, PIC ADVISOR:

Since the arriving day to this province up to date, he has shown proof of good will and outstanding advisor. He launched the DIA PHONG campaign in this province and gave it a very effective support, resulted over 300 overt and covert VCI were neutralized.

Beside that, MR KELLY also was a brave advisor. He participated in many Police and PHUNG HOANG OPERATIONS, particularly on 26 May 70 he conducted a National Police Field Force Platoon to operate at PHU DANG hamlet, THANH THOI village, Mo Cay district, resulting in 5 VC killed, 1 3A1 sub machine gun, two anti tank mines and many ammunitions of all types were seized.

With the above brilliant feats, I would like to propose you to award him a Cross of Gallantry with Bronze Star Medal (commended before Regiment) on the occasion of his transfer to another province in July 1970.

2-Mr Pham Van Dien, Assistant PIC Advisor:

Side by side with Mr Kelly in all missions, Mr Pham Van Dien has a special talent to proselyte ex VC cadre to work for the Dai Phong campaign. He also provides to PHUNG HOANG COMMITTEE many good information to eliminate VCI.

For this reason, I would like to propose you to award him a Certificate.

```
                              Kien Hoa, 26 June 1970
                              Major Ho Van Man
                              Phung Hoang Center Chief
                                  S/S
```

Ben R. Games, PhD

COMBAT MEDICAL REPORT #1
Joseph B. Kelly

Enemy attack on US Embassy 7/8 June 1970

Documents Attached:

1. MACV Embassy Dispensary, Medical Report dated 16 June 1970.

2. Letter of Appreciation from Major Geoffrey T. Barker, Infantry dated at 2 February 1984.

3. Official Superior's Report of Injury.
   1st dtd Monday, 8th June 1970. 10 days after the attack on the Embassy.
   2nd dtd Tuesday, 22 Sept 1970. Shortly after attack. (less than 1 hour)

. Copy of Supervisors Report (not signed) indicating where records of the attack were filed and classified secret.

5. Picture of roof over American Embassy quarters of Joseph B. Kelly taken from manuscript of "Confession of a CIA Interrogator" by Ben R. Games, PhD, author.

I hereby certify that the information I have given in the non-fiction story "Confession of a CIA Interrogator", this statement, and documents are true to the best of my knowledge and belief.

For God & Country,

Joseph B. Kelly, SSN#214-26-7549
10141 Flagstone Road
Brooksville, FL 34601

True Copy

Phone #352-796-9793

A Cry for Help

WITHOUT PREJUDICE

Mr. John L. Kiener, Editor
Herald & Tribune PO Box 277
Jonesborough, TN 37659

19 Jan 1991
Phone 1-413-753-3136

Ref: Review of "Confessions of a CIA Interrogator by Ben R. Games, PhD".

Dear John,

I've known Joe Kelly since 1949 when he was taking care of my survival equipment and parachute on Naha, Okinawa. At that time I was flying a P-61 Black Widow on night intruder missions along the coast of China.

One weekend when Joe and I were visiting after flying our powered parachutes he asked me how I felt about what we had done in Vietnam. Then he gave me some secret documents to take home and read. I never write about a subject unless I can verify it as true from two different sources. Joe had the documents that did this only I couldn't use them. I agreed to write Joe's biography of his 2½ years in Vietnam, so Gilbert became all the contract CIA Agents I've known.

I changed the lead character in the story to the CIA Pseudonym Gilbert H. Moriggia which Joe identified as his code name. I couldn't find a ID or SS number for Gilbert but I discovered the name had once been used by the OSS during WWII. I would write a Chapter of the book and then send it to Joe for proof reading. Each chapter was then individually Copyrighted. I also made arrangements for Joe to buy books from my publisher at bookstore prices.

I don't remember but I may not have told Joe that after I was released from the hospital at Fort Rucker a B/General and an Intelligent officer would fly from Paris to Maxwell Air Force base and brief me on the proposals that the Americans were going to make at the Paris Peace Accord. The Army would later fly me to Washington D.C. where I briefed the Senate Armed Service Committee and the Joint Chiefs of Staff on how the North Vietnamese were going to act at the meeting.

If you are quoting from the book "Confession of a CIA Interrogator" and really need to know the individuals I'm writing about ask Joe. In the story I

Ben R. Games, PhD

never refer to any papers marked secret except Joe's medical records of combat injuries. The FBI, the Secret Service, and the CIA performed security clearance checks before the story was printed. I've done this type of writing for our government since high school. Once the CIA commissioned a Professor of English to review my writing. She wrote that my writing was juvenile and a person with a third grade level of reading would understand it. She also gave examples. I got the job.

The Commander of the Navy Seal Team that helped Joe was a personal friend, and I promised not to use any of their names in the story. Helen and I were invited to the change of Command Ceremony in San Diego when he was promoted to Navy Captain. There were three Navy Seals in his team that were awarded the Medal of Honor in Vietnam but their names are secret.

Joe may have told you that we are members of the LDS or Mormon church and that I have been a councilor in the Branch Presidency. I grew up at Lee's Ferry, Arizona and Hurricane, Utah. We, Helen my wife for the past 67 years, and I were married in the Temple at Salt Lake City.

I enjoy reading about your review of the Book "Confession of a CIA Interrogator." I really enjoyed how you gasped how I introduced Joe into the story as Gilbert. It was a real and much appreciated complement especially coming from a professional writer like yourself. Now setback into your chair and just take another long look at the book. Not a professional cover, misspelled words, typing errors and self published. It's got to have been written by a layman.

I once wrote a story about Santa Clause. The story was about a lost letter from the leader of the PDM action committee who were trying to get control of their government. According to the story he wrote a letter to Santa telling him about the problem. Somehow I got confused and thought his committee was part of the government. After they flew into Miami I met them in Naples, Fl for a lunch meeting. I gave each person a copy of my working manuscript. When Super "C" read the letter with his signature he stopped and read it again. Then he challenged me asking how I had got Santa to give me a copy of <u>his</u> letter. The story was approved, and I got to pay the check.

                For God and Country,

G Dr. Ben R. Games, PhD
    814 Church St # 102
    Ellenton, FL 34222-2318

A Cry for Help

VETERANS ADMINISTRATION
REGIONAL OFFICE
P.O. BOX 1437
ST. PETERSBURG, FLORIDA 33731

Date: June 15, 1978
In Reply Refer to: 317/21
C 15 227 804

Mr. Ben R. Games
6445 Lake Sunrise Drive
Apollo Beach, FL 33570

Your claim for disability compensation has been considered on the basis of all the evidence, including reports received from the Service Department. The evidence establishes service connection for the following conditions evaluated as shown:

Condition	Percent of Disability
Splenectomy	30%
Postoperative hiatal hernia and post-operative gallbladder	10%
Arthritis	10%
Right inguinal hernia and postoperative repair, bilateral	0% (see attached)

The evidence does not show service connection for the following:

Because you may not receive full payment of service retired pay and VA compensation at the same time, we have no choice but to disallow your claim. However, you may waive a portion of your retired pay and elect to receive VA compensation instead, in the amount(s) and from the date(s) shown below:

Degree of Disability	Monthly Payment	Commencing Date
40%	$155.00	1-1-78

You may make the waiver by completing and returning the enclosed VA Form 21-651 within one year from the date of this letter. Before you decide, please read the instructions and information on the back of this letter.

If you elect VA compensation (as your greater benefit), we will deduct the amount of retired pay you have already received beginning with the commencing date shown above. If your retired pay is greater than VA compensation and you waive that portion equal to the payment shown, your VA compensation payment will begin on the date of reduction of your retired pay.

If you believe our decision is incorrect, please see the enclosure which explains your procedural and appeal rights.

ADJUDICATION OFFICER

Encl. VA Forms 21-651
  VA Form 1-4107
  VA Form 22-1900; FL 22-339   (Over)

FL 21-826
FEB 1976(RS)

"To care for him who shall have borne the battle, and for his widow, and his orphan." – ABRAHAM LINCOLN

Ben R. Games, PhD

Handwritten note at top: Given to me by VA Dr. Royalty Garner, MD. FAP officer 24 Oct 2004. I collect and read it but it may be important. ~ Ben

GAMES, BEN R (317-18-1165)

Exam Date/Time:
03/27/2004 10:42

Procedure Name:
SPINE LUMBOSACRAL MIN 4 VIEWS

Clinical History:
c/o low back pain, s/p ground level fall x3 days ago

Impression:
1. Interval appearance of minimal loss of stature of the L3 vertebral body predominantly secondary to depression of the superior vertebral endplate. The age of this is indeterminate but could be recent. Clinical correlation is suggested.

2. All of the lumbar vertebral bodies are fairly well aligned. The remaining lumbar vertebral bodies are of normal height.

3. Moderate narrowing of the L4-L5 intervertebral disk space and marked narrowing of the L5-S1 intervertebral disk space.

4. Multi-level mild lumbar spondylosis.

5. Reidentified multiple metallic surgical sutures projecting in the midline extending from the lower visualized thoracic spine down to the upper sacrum with many of the sutures broken.

6. Reidentified status post bilateral total hip arthroplasties.

7. The pedicles appear intact.

8. Stat reading. Dr. Shaver, emergency room physician, notified about radiographic findings.

9. A view alert was placed on this report. GAMES,BEN/317181165 D: 03/27/04 14:41 T: 03/28/04 12:44 TSI# R112 JOB# 2366082

Report:
CASE #9415, LUMBOSACRAL SPINE, AP, LATERAL, AND FOCUSED LATERAL VIEWS, ON PACS, DATED 3/27/04.

COMPARISON: AP supine abdomen, on PACS, dated 5/28/97 demonstrating the lumbosacral spine in the AP projection.

FINDINGS: See impression below.

Facility:
TAMPA VAMC

Handwritten note at bottom: Games the Aircraft Commander. Upon crashing, the helicopter cyclic jammed into his Bullet Board Armor and ruptured his spleen, cracked two ribs, and caused a lung to collapse with a hiatal hernia. The lung was re-inflated by drawing blood ten hours after the firefight at Phuoc Phunk Hospital. Hips replaced by VA hospital. ~ Ben R. Games

DR. BEN R. GAMES PhD.

A Cry for Help

X ~~*Ben R. Games*~~
SIGNATURE OF VETERAN

X ~~*signature*~~
DIRECTOR BENEFITS AND ASSISTANCE DIVISION

Florida Department of Veterans' Affairs
9500 Bay Pines Boulevard, Room 214
Bay Pines, Florida 33744

www.FloridaVets.org

FLORIDA DEPARTMENT OF VETERANS' AFFAIRS

15 227 804
Ben R. Games
814 Church St #102
Ellenton, FL 34222

Height: 5'9"   Weight: 205   DOB: 05/05/24

100% Service Connected Permanently and Totally Disabled Veteran

Ben R. Games, PhD

Mr. Bill Moor
South Bend Tribune Writer
223 W. Colfax Avenue
South Bend, Indiana 46626   27 June 2005

Dear Bill,

This is permission for you to use any of my writings, information contained there in, or medical records obtained from any source in your article for the South Bend Tribune.

If there is any questions you would like to ask please do so. It is true I have been trying to use my combat record and some times misadventures to help the Vietnam Veterans. This was the war where the Communist convinced Americans that it cost too much to save the Vietnamese people. It was the last war where the enemy identified them selves and fought on a common battle field. Once the American people understand that the Vietnam Veterans have suffered more for our country than the citizen soldiers of any war they will never let this happen again. It is one thing to put your life on the line with the support of the American people but to do it and have them hate you for dieing is a sure way to lose our freedom.

Mr. Carl Lau, owner of Airlief Publishing, Martinsville, IN Ph: 800-342-6068 has notified me that Fox Studios, and other TV producers have displayed an interest in my latest book: "Confession of a CIA Interrogator".
It is a Non-Fiction account of 2 and ½ years of a contract CIA employee. Mr. Joseph B. Kelly, GS-11. We have flown together for many years, and our paths crossed in Okinawa, Japan, France, and of course in Vietnam.

The manuscript is finished, and I am looking for a publisher who is interested in this type of work.

For God and Country,

DR. BEN R. GAMES

A Cry for Help

Mr. Vin Mannx
The Herald Tribune
PO Box #921
Bradenton, FL 34206

28 June 2005

Question: Can a Terrorist Organization successfully attack the Veteran Administration Computer & Records system?

Dear Sir;

This is one time I hope and pray that I am wrong but if the VA Rating Decision letter (12/17/04) # 15-227-804 is based upon information in their computer files, then somehow a Terrorist Organization may have successfully compromised the computer program and medical records. If it is not from an attack by terrorist then someone in the Veterans Administration should know how to correct the problem.

The war in Iraq is proving once again that Citizen Soldiers are the back bone of our military. History is a window that looks into the future. Even our children know that without the National Guard and Military Reserves serving overseas the terrorist attacks could be happening in Bradenton or in hometowns throughout America. As long as we remember them old citizen soldiers never die but just fade away into history as we enjoy the freedom they fought for.

Remember the Vietnam War? The men and women who fought in that war sure do. They will attest that we never lost a battle but were defeated on the home front. Is it possible that the terrorist have studied history and learned how the communist used our thirst for knowledge to sabotage the will to toe the line until victory? If the errors found in the VA Computer files is the work of terrorist then our country is in great trouble. If it is by incompetence then we the people are at fault for letting it happen.

I am proud to be counted as one of these veteran citizen soldiers and defenders of our homeland. The VA has written records showing overseas service in WWII, Korea, The Berlin Crises, and the Vietnam war with injuries caused by the enemy during combat along with medals issued for heroism and valor. None of these records seem to be recorded in the VA

Ben R. Games, PhD

computer. Medical decisions based upon false or misleading information are not only dangerous but can create mistrust of the entire VA system.

When the Veteran Administration informed me that their records indicated that I had never served in combat during war time I asked our congresswomen Katherine Harris to assist them in correcting the computer records. She was informed by a letter from VA Region Director Mr. R.F. Bowron stating that I was only interested in more money from my injuries, and I was also against some veterans bill or law. He never addressed the question of the lost records or screwed up computer files.

The Honorable Senator Mel Martinez wrote informing me that the VA was going to check into the changed computer records but that they had not set a time when the investigations would start. Then I wrote the President my Commander In-Chief asking for someone to assist the VA, and this letter was forwarded to the Veterans Administration. It was a little like asking the fox who was guarding the chicken coop.

I can understand if the Veterans Administration is only covering-up while the FBI or Homeland Defense is investigating and trying to locate the person or terrorist responsible. I am over 81, and do have one question. If I die before they locate the terrorist will the person be charged with murder or just for trying to destroy the moral of a citizen soldier?

Sincerely;

DR. BEN R. GAMES PhD.

A Cry for Help

The Honorable Mel Martinez
Attn: Staff Assistant Marie Tillery
315 E. Robinson St, Landmark Center 1
Orlando, FL 33281

17 August 2005

Ref: Phone conversation 15 August 2005. Purple Heart

Dear Marie,

It was a pleasure speaking with you today. I know you didn't ask but just to let you know my heart is in the right place... I'm a life member of the RNC & Senate Inter Circle. Please thank Senator Martinez for allowing you to help me.

As per your request; On the 8th November 1968 I was an Aircraft Commander CH-47 Chinook helicopter hit by enemy fire over LZ Vivian, Vietnam in the republic of Vietnam. During the firefight the helicopter was engulfed in flames and the starboard engine shot off. The helicopter was destroyed in the battle. I received the DFC for heroism for my actions in the firefight.

Due to the sever trauma from the crash I receive a Hiatal Hernia, ruptured spleen, various internal ruptures, and damage to both hips and back. Both hips were diagnosed as having DJD, statis post bilateral total hip replacement. After returning to Ft Rucker Hospital I received a complete body fluoroscope and x-rays. The internal damage was not repaired at this time.

In November 1973 I was admitted to the Wright Patterson AFB hospital and administered 4 units of blood. A complete workup was done but no repairs made.

In April 1976 I was operated on at Mac Dill AFB Hospital. My spleen removed, Hiatal Hernia & diaphragm repaired along with other ruptures. I was told that my injuries were caused by sever trauma, and the damage had not shown up on the x-rays. After retirement my ruptures were repaired by the VA.

Ben R. Games Ph.D.
814 Church St.
Ellenton, FL 34222

Ben R. Games, PhD

The American Legion
Mr. John Zangas
1608 "K" Street, N.W.
Washington DC 20006-2847   20 August 2005

Ref: Military Review Boards Hearing, Life member Ben R. Games, PhD, SSN 1165, Dept: FL, Post 400, #201924710, yrs (8). VA File #15 227 804.

Dear John,

As per letter request to keep your office informed about actions regarding correcting of the VA computer files and medical records for presentation to the review board is as follows.

I had requested Representative Harris to ask the Veterans Administration, St Petersburg Regional Office to correct their computer records to reflect the DD214 issued at time of my military retirement. I was informed by phone on 22nd July 05 from Staff Assistant Mr. Adam Chandler that the VA had changed and corrected their files to show my actual active duty to be over 27 years. He informed me that the VA would not notify anyone that the records had been corrected at it would indicate that all their decision based upon this clear and unmistakable error were not correct.

I have written VA Director Mr. R.F. Bowron thanking him for correcting the VA Computer files. I have not yet received an acknowledgement of the corrections but I do believe that our congresswoman wouldn't try to fool me. The VA may have already corrected my combat injuries to reflect the actually cause, I keep hoping that they will admit that the mistakes happened and help clean up my records. I admit that if it wasn't for the Veterans Administrations help I wouldn't have been able to toe the line for all these years. They should be proud.

Please send copies of these letters to the Correction Review Board if they are needed.

Sincerely,

DR. BEN R. GAMES PhD.

A Cry for Help

General Robert V. Taylor
Chairman of the Board, NGAUS
Washington DC 20001   4 July 2005
                 Ref: THE FIGHT AHEAD

Dear Bob,

In the fight ahead when you are undecided on the course to follow just remember that history is a window looking into the future. We are living in a GEO Feudal Age. Instead of kings, we have chairman of the board, instead of knights there are Generals, Instead of surfs, we have workers, and instead of peasants, there are stockholders.

In medieval times, it was the same as today. The army with the citizen soldiers is the winner. We need professional soldiers but they need the citizen soldiers or all they can due is win battles but the war will be lost. Vietnam was a perfect example of how to win battles and lose a war.

After I returned from Vietnam to Michigan in 1970, I was sent TDY to Fort Rucker to attend The US Army Aviation Warrant Officers Career Course (Advanced) so I could blend in as a National Guard Warrant Officer. What you may not have known was that my other job was writing opinion letters for the Paris Peace Talks on how the North Vietnamese would respond to our proposals. Besides briefing the Joint Chiefs and the Senate Armed Services Committee during 1970 & 1971, I worked as one of your recruiters.

In 1947 while in the Army's General Hospital, Battle Creek recovering from exposure of Ionizing Radiation I wrote that an Atomic attack on the US would not cripple us until after 1975. We were dispersed with military units and weapons in armories through out the land. In the 1950, my thesis was on the type of tactics and weapons needed for the defense of our cities. I also co-authored a paper using pressures instead of vacuum to simulate space for training purposes. In the 1960 at the USAF Air University, it was how to clean up after an accidental explosion of an atomic device.

Our country must never make military target large or big enough that one attack will cause us to stop fighting. If our enemies in Iraq make this mistake, the world will be missing a lot of terrorist tomorrow.

                                           DR. BEN R. GAMES PhD.

Ben R. Games, PhD

DECODING

CRSC File #28765

Department of Veterans Affairs
Letter dtd 6 September 2005
317/VSC/PRE1/CD, Games, Ben R.

The Veterans Administration made a decision on the 17 December 2004 based upon a Clear and Unmistakable Errors in their Computer Files. The undersigned requested a VA Decision Review Officer (DRO) officer be assigned and an Appeals Board review the Errors in the VA records.

The VA had miss posted or did not understand how to read the DD214, the DD759, and military awards for heroism issued at retirement. There is another possibility. Some terrorist may have compromised the VA computer to discredit them and attack our citizen soldiers.

Attached is a letter from the Veterans Administration dated 6 September 2005. They have corrected part of the computer files and are attempting to verify another gap in their records. The US Army Physical Disability Agency (CRSC) has requested information from the VA for their reason and documentation in assigning Non Combat Disability Codes for combat injuries.

The VA letter does not give a reason or the documentation requested, but did state that their records indicate that 24 yrs. 4 ms. 4 da. of active duty have been verified. The letter stated that they were still attempting to verify the period of active service 10/01/1962 - 07/01/1973. Using the Freedom of Information Act the undersigned reviewed the VA files and discovered the information needed to verify this period. As a guide please note the following:

    1. 1962 stationed Chambley Air Base France, Berlin Crises, family live in base housing, military rank, Major USAF. Non flying.

    2. 1964 Bunker Hill AFB, IN. reinstated as pilot, Major USAF.

The Conspiracy to Change History

3. 1965 USAF Recruiting Service & Solo Artic Circle Flight.

4. 1966 USAF Investigating Officer for recruiter misconduct & pilot violation of flying regulations. Major USAF.

5. 1967 Thailand Marine Police, Major USAF Instructor for LA-4. 1967, Detroit Riots, pilot CH-19 for General Ward, conditional release from USAF assigned to MI Army National Guard. CW-2.

6. 1968, Ft Rucker, Al. Active duty Army Aviator qualification Courses for H-13, UH-1, CH-47, Helicopter Instrument School, and fix wing aircraft.

7. 1969, 1st Cavalry Division, 228 Av Bn, Co. B, Bear Cat, Vietnam, CW-3, awarded 13 Air Medals, and DFC for heroism.

8. 1970, "E" BT, 82 Artillery, 1st Cavalry Division, Phouc Vinh, Vietnam, CW-3. Awarded the Bronze Star.

9. 1971, Ft Rucker, AL. Advanced Aviation Warrant Officer Career Course, CW-4.

10. 1972, Active Duty Recruiting Service MI ARNG, Michigan.

I hereby certify that the information I have given is true to the best of my belief and knowledge.

Sincerely,

Dr. Ben R. Games, PhD
814 Church St # 102
Ellenton, FL 34222

Ben R. Games, PhD

Congresswoman Katherine Harris
Staff Assistant Ms. Casey Prescott
1112 Manatee Ave W. Suite #902
Bradenton, FL 34205

9 September 2005

Ref: Request for the Honorable Katherine to issue statements to the VA Decision Review Officer (DRO) concerning an Appeal of the VA Decision 12/17/04, Veteran Ben R. Games File #15 227 804.

Dear Casey,

As I told you in our conversation today I was both pleased and upset when Adam informed me by phone that the Veterans Administration had corrected their computer files to show my active duty service, and combat injuries. Happy that the record had been corrected but unhappy that they had not issued a written correction letter. When I asked Adam if the VA had apologized for the misinformation that they had given to Congresswomen Harris he said that they had and your office was satisfied.

On the 6th of September 2005 I learned from a VA letter that Adam had only been told part of the truth. The phone call was designed to satisfy the Honorable Congresswoman that all was well with the VA.

They really need help. If the VA Administrators can misinform congress and change records for someone with my service record then they must be really doing a job on the Veterans who can not fight back.

For God and Country,

DR. BEN R. GAMES PhD.

A Cry for Help

Honorable Steve Buyer
Chairman, VA Committee
Washington D.C. 20515   15 September 2005

Ref: Compromised VA Computer Files #15 227 804, Games, Ben R.

Dear Sir;

I discovered quit by accident that some of my VA medical records had been changed or lost due to the Veterans Administration computer files being compromised either by terrorist or incompetence. Whatever the reason a VA Service Representative informed me that the computer records could not be corrected without the help of VFW Service Officer Mr. Kenneth Thie, at the VA St Petersburg Regional Office. I wrote the VFW requesting that he assist the VA on 1 June 2005.

Mr. Kenneth Thie not only agreed to assist them but he responded quickly. I received a phone call and a letter from the Veterans Administration on the 6 September 2005 showing that most of the errors had been corrected. Mr. Thai refused to take credit for his work and acted like solving this type of a problem was an everyday occurrence. I have been a supporter and life member of the VFW since 1967. I just wanted you to know that many people and organizations are supporting you and the work of your committee.

              Sincerely;

Copy of VA letter   DR. BEN R. GAMES PhD.
& My answer.

Ben R. Games, PhD

Manatee County Veterans Services
Mr. Hal Willis Jr, Services Specialist
Post Office Box 1000
Bradenton, FL 34206   14 October 2005

Ref: Your letter dtd 4 April 2005. Veteran Service.

Dear Hal,

I'm sorry to take so long to write a rebuttal to your letter. The VA had to provide the information to refute some of your arguments in the letter.

You are correct the VA only classifies injuries as service connected or non-service connected. I was wrong to assume otherwise. In my defense the Army CRSC had asked the Veterans Administration by letter on 12/02/04 for their supporting documents for VA codes #7706, 7346, and 5003. The Army Physical Disability Agency is only trying to discover if the VA treated me for trauma that wasn't due to combat. The VA responded on the 6 September 2005 stating that they had verified over 24 years active military service except for the period 10/01/1962 to 07/01/1973 (Vietnam Era).

I spoke to the VA DRO Officer investigating my VA Claim, and she informed me that the VA has not conceded that I was in Vietnam. Senator Martinez had a Staff Assistant phone me and I quote her, "The VA uses the term Era to indicate that someone served during a period but may not have actually been there".

Someone changed the VA classification for the bilateral hip replacements to non-service connected to match their Computer Records. I have agreed in writing to waiver any VA benefit payments if they correct their records.

You may want to attend my VA Appeals hearing as a representative for all Manatee Veterans. It's about my appeal, but also about the VA Computer Files being compromised or incompetence that effects all county veterans.

                                    Sincerely,

                                                                    DR. BEN R. GAMES PhD.

A Cry for Help

DEPARTMENT OF ...
ARMY REVIEW BOARDS AGENCY
1901 SOUTH BELL STREET
ARLINGTON VA 22202-4508

November 17, 2005

SFMR-RBR-ST/wa
AR20050007776

BEN R. GAMES, LTC-RETIRED
814 CHURCH ST
ELLENTON FL 34222

Dear Colonel Games:

    This is in response to your application to the Army Board For Correction of Military Records (ABCMR) dated April 27, 2005. It appears you are asking the ABCMR for assistance with decisions made by the Department of Veterans Administration (VA).

    I understand how frustrating your situation must be for you, but we must advise you that the ABCMR has no control or influence over the administration of the VA and its decisions. The VA operates under its own laws, rules, and regulations. Since you apparently have not received satisfaction from the VA, you may wish to understand the VA appeal process or seek assistance through your congressperson or senator. Those representatives strive to assist their constituency whenever possible.

    In view of the foregoing, the ABCMR has asked me to file your application without action and without prejudice. The ABCMR has not denied your application. If you identify an injustice or error in your Army records you may reapply to the ABCMR for consideration.

    I trust that this information is helpful.

                      Sincerely,

                      Victor D. Whitney
                      Chief, Case Management Division

Ben R. Games, PhD

Department of the Army
Victor D. Whitney, Chief
Army Review Board Agency
1901 South Bell Street
Arlington, VA 22202-4508 23 November 2005

Ref: SFMR-RBR-AT/wa, AR20050007776, Ben R. Games. Letter 11/17/05.

Dear Sir;

Thank you for your signed letter with notification that my application is being held without prejudice or action.

The ABCMR Board is correct I was asking for a ruling to assist me in proving that the VA computer records and files have been compromised by someone. Please give the board my apology as it was wrong to involve them, but when I'm fighting for our country I'll take any help available. Also I wanted the VA to save face and fire the persons or person responsible without a lot of fanfare. Three years ago it was suggested that I check on my VA medical records to see if they matched the actual files. Someone must have suspected that the VA was being attacked. I accepted in the belief that the VA is the backbone of our citizen soldiers, and must be protected against terrorists. Also my military records and combat awards for heroism are will documented. This was going to be a piece of cake, I thought.

I've found that some VA records were changed, some missing, and their computer files were completely messed up. For some reason the VA is covering for someone. It's hard to pinpoint an individual because no one will sign a VA letter (all are hand stamped signatures).

Thank you for the suggestion on using a congressperson or senator to assist in the fight to save the VA. So far one congressperson assistant and one Senatorial assistant have left for other work. When the VA twists the truth to a congressperson or senator they do not like it, but the VA has a lot of power and long memory. This is my problem to solve. The VA expects that I will die before they have to correct their files. If they are right then I hereby pass the gauntlet to your Board Members to stand for our warriors.

Sincerely;

DR. BEN R. GAMES PhD.

A Cry for Help

DEPARTMENT OF THE ARMY
U.S. ARMY PHYSICAL DISABILITY AGENCY
COMBAT-RELATED SPECIAL COMPENSATION (CRSC)
200 STOVALL STREET
ALEXANDRIA, VIRGINIA 22332-0470

REPLY TO
ATTENTION OF

November 30, 2006

Combat-Related Special
Compensation Division

Re: Claim Number <u>91210</u>

MAJ (RET) Ben R. Games (SSN: 317-18-1165)
814 Church St.
Ellenton, FL 34222

VA COPY
Please send this copy to your
servicing Veterans Administration

Dear MAJ Games (Retired):

"You may be due benefits from Veterans Administration (VA) previously withheld by them due to your receipt of retired pay. You must send the enclosed copy of this letter to VA to enable VA to determine if additional benefits are payable. This letter contains essential information regarding your CRSC decision needed by VA to determine entitlement."

- Per DOD/VA Directive

CRSC Determination:

Based on the documentation you provided to verify your claim, your request for CRSC reconsideration has been approved. A copy of this letter has been forwarded to the Defense Finance and Accounting Service (DFAS) for further processing. DFAS should initiate your payment within 60 days of the date of this letter. CRSC payments will be made in the same manner as your retired pay. DFAS will review your pay account information and may change the payment effective date based on your particular pay account history. All payment inquires after 60 days should be addressed to DFAS and not CRSC.

Verified as Combat-Related Illnesses/Injuries:

We were able to find evidence to verify the following illnesses/injuries as being linked to a combat-related situation.

VA Disability Code	VA Description	VA Percent Disability	CRSC Eligibility Determination	Effective Date
7706	Removal of Spleen	30%	Yes - IN	20040101
6602	Asthma	10%	Yes - IN	20040401
7306	Marginal Ulcer	10%	Yes - IN	20040101 - 20040331
7306	Marginal Ulcer	40%	Yes - IN	20040401
6602	Asthma	0%	Yes - IN	20040101 - 20040331

CRSC Form 11
CRSC Original and Reconsideration Split Approval Letter
November 30, 2006

Ben R. Games, PhD

MAJ (RET) Ben R. Games (SSN: 317-18-1165)

Verified as Combat-Related Illnesses/Injuries: (cont'd)

VA Disability Code	VA Description	VA Percent Disability	CRSC Eligibility Determination	Effective Date
5297	Removal of Rib(S)	0%	Yes - IN	20040101

- Total Combat Related Disability: 40%   Effective 20040101 - 20040331
- Total Combat Related Disability: 60%   Effective 20040401 - Present

☒ This service member has Individual Unemployment Compensation: IU, Effective 20040401

☒ This service member is not receiving Special Monthly Compensation.

Unable to Verify as Combat-Related Illnesses/Injuries:

We were unable to find any official 'documentary evidence' to verify the following service-related illnesses/injuries as combat-related.

VA Disability Code	VA Description	VA Percent Disability
5010	Traumatic Arthritis	10%
5201	Limited Motion of Arm	0%

Reconsideration Request:

We encourage you to go through your personal/personnel and Veterans Administration (VA) medical records to look for any evidence we can use to make the link between a combat-related situation and your service related Illnesses/Injuries. If you do not have copies of documentation "stating how you got the injury" then there are several ways you can recreate records to support this claim. As a courtesy, we have enclosed a copy of our education slides and Frequently Asked Questions (FAQ), which explains some ways to recreate lost or undocumented records. Please keep in mind that the Department of Defense (DOD) guidelines of this program prohibit us from using personal or buddy statements to validate this claim. To apply for reconsideration, please fill out the enclosed CRSC form 12e and send us the additional supporting documentation that verifies your claim. Please allow us 60 business days to process your reconsideration request. Your claim number is 91210; please refer to this claim number on all correspondence.

ARBA Correction of Personnel Records:

CRSC Form 11
CRSC Original and Reconsideration Split Approval Letter
November 30, 2006

A Cry for Help

MAJ (RET) Ben R. Games (SSN: 317-18-1165)

If you feel that there is an error in your personnel records which is causing your case to be disapproved (i.e. you served in Vietnam but there is no record of this combat service on your DD214) then you can apply for a correction of your military records using the enclosed DD form 149. Mail the form and the supporting documents to:

>Department of Army Review Boards Agency
>Attn: Assistant Operations Officer
>Jefferson Davis Highway 2nd Floor
>Arlington, VA 22203-4508
>http://arba.army.pentagon.mil/

Thank you for your dedicated service and sacrifices. Our goal is to serve you the Veteran.

FOR THE DIVISION CHIEF:

Sincerely,

Mistie Kay Wisniewski
W01, US Army
Combat Related Special Compensation

Enclosures

CRSC Form 11
CRSC Original and Reconsideration Split Approval Letter
November 30, 2006

Ben R. Games, PhD

DEPARTMENT OF THE ARMY
U.S. ARMY PHYSICAL DISABILITY AGENCY
COMBAT-RELATED SPECIAL COMPENSATION (CRSC)
200 STOVALL STREET
ALEXANDRIA, VIRGINIA 22332-0470

REPLY TO
ATTENTION OF

Combat-Related Special
Compensation Division

To Veterans Administration (VA) or Local Military Treatment Facility (MTF) Doctor:

This retired veteran has submitted a claim for benefits under the Combat-Related Special Compensation (CRSC) program and has not been able to produce evidence that we can use to substantiate the claim. DOD guidelines do not allow us to accept personal or buddy statements and only allow us to use official documentary evidence (i.e. VA decisions, sick call slips, letters, or consultation documents from their doctor at an MTF or the VA medical facilities). The purpose of this letter is to explain the intent of your patients' appointment.

The number one reason CRSC denies a claim is due to a lack of combat-related evidence supporting that injury or illness. We do not possess the official documentation that tells us "how" the veteran got the injury/illness. It is our hope that as a medical professional you are able to assist by going through this veteran's medical history and proof, to verify how the injury or illness was incurred. We have been informed by the VA and by medical professionals that if the retiree is able to provide the VA or primary care doctor at a local military treatment facility (MTF) with their current medical documentation, proof of assignment when injury occurred (i.e. 2-1/2A orders, NCOERS, OERS or anything else to prove assignment to injury timing), their personal history statement, and possibly a buddy statement, then the VA or MTF doctor *may* be able to attribute the injury or illness to a combat-related incident. If the doctor is willing to document a simple medical consultation form or a letter that states "how" the injury was incurred, then we are authorized to use such documentation to substantiate this claim.

Under the CRSC program, a combat-related injury or illness can be any injury or illness that results by the means of **Hazardous Service (HS)** (i.e. aerial flight, parachute duty, demolition duty, experimental stress duty, and diving duty); **Simulations of War (SW)** (i.e. FTX, Special Forces training exercises, combat confidence course or lanes training, or other named training exercises which are used to prepare for combat); injury or illness incurred by **Instrumentalities of War (IN)** (i.e. tanks, Agent Orange, grenade simulators, military planes, and other items unique to the military); and of course, injuries or illnesses which are the result of **Armed Combat (AC)** - directly or indirectly (i.e. Purple Heart (PH) injuries or secondary conditions as a result of the injury).

Thank you for helping us to reward our Retired Veterans the benefits they have earned.

John F. Sackett
Colonel, U.S. Army
Chief, Combat-Related
Special Compensation Division

See attached sample letter.

CRSC Form 22
CRSC Doctor Support Letter

US Army CRSC Agency
200 Stovall Street
Alexandria, VA 22332-0470

Sample

Ben R. Games, Major US Army Retired, VA File Number C15 227 804, CRSC Claim # 91210.

Anyone falling from 800 feet and hitting the ground while in a seated position would have damage to their hips and spine. The veteran reported that the other pilot received a back injury during the combat action, but that the troopers who were standing trying to avoid the flames were able to continue fighting. VA records indicate that the helicopter came under enemy fire on the approach to LZ Vivian 8 November 1969.

The veteran spleen was ruptured, two ribs cracked, hiatal hernia, and a lung collapsed as a result of the cyclic stick hitting his chest in the crash. VA Decision letter dated 3 October 2006 documents that Ben R. Games, VA Fife Number C15 227 804 is a Combat Veteran and the provisions of 38 CFR 3.304 (d) apply.

Sample

Please mail to Veteran so it can be included with other VA letters attached to CRSC claim form.

Ben R. Games

Ben R. Games PhD
814 Church St # 102
Ellenton, FL 34222-2318

Colonial Williamsburg Foundation

Ben R. Games, PhD

DEPARTMENT OF ...
ARMY REVIEW BOARDS AGENCY
1901 SOUTH BELL STREET
ARLINGTON VA 22202-4508

November 17, 2005

SFMR-RBR-ST/wa
AR20050007776

BEN R. GAMES, LTC-RETIRED
814 CHURCH ST
ELLENTON FL 34222

Dear Colonel Games:

    This is in response to your application to the Army Board For Correction of Military Records (ABCMR) dated April 27, 2005. It appears you are asking the ABCMR for assistance with decisions made by the Department of Veterans Administration (VA).

    I understand how frustrating your situation must be for you, but we must advise you that the ABCMR has no control or influence over the administration of the VA and its decisions. The VA operates under its own laws, rules, and regulations. Since you apparently have not received satisfaction from the VA, you may wish to understand the VA appeal process or seek assistance through your congressperson or senator. Those representatives strive to assist their constituency whenever possible.

    In view of the foregoing, the ABCMR has asked me to file your application without action and without prejudice. The ABCMR has not denied your application. If you identify an injustice or error in your Army records you may reapply to the ABCMR for consideration.

    I trust that this information is helpful.

                              Sincerely,

                              Victor D. Whitney
                              Chief, Case Management Division

A Cry for Help

DEPARTMENT OF VETERANS AFFAIRS
Regional Office
P. O. Box 1437
St. Petersburg, FL 33731

NOV 3 0 2005
DR. BEN R GAMES
814 CHURCH ST
ELLENTON, FL 34222

In Reply Refer To:
317/CONG/ERR
C 15 227 804
GAMES, Ben R.

Dear Dr. Games:

    This is in reply to your letter of November 24, 2005, sent to President George W. Bush. We are writing to you because our office has jurisdiction of your Department of Veterans Affairs (VA) claims folder. We apologize for the delay in responding to your letters.

    We will associate your letter with your claims folder. We certainly do not want to discredit your statement of the length of time serving in the military. Our records indicate you have twenty years, ten months of active service and fourteen years, five months of inactive service. Also, our records do not indicate active service from 1962 - 1973. We have requested verification of active service from 1962 – 1973 from the military to verify your statement. If you have discharge papers in that regard, please send VA a copy. We will send you a copy of the service medical records at a later date.

    VA only provides the Army with the details of your VA compensation and injuries including a copy of your service medical records. The Army makes the decision regarding CRSC. It is in your best interest to contact the Department of the Army to dispute your issue. If you feel there are additional conditions not presently acknowledged as service connected, or even conditions secondary to a service connected disability, we encourage you to file a claim with the assistance of your designated Veterans Service Organization, The Disabled American Veterans. Any additional disabilities as a result of a new claim are reportable to the Army.

    We are sorry that we cannot provide you with a more favorable response to your inquiry at this time.

    If you have additional questions or concerns, please feel free to visit our office located at 9500 Bay Pines Blvd., Bay Pines, FL 33744 or telephone toll-free 1-800-827-1000. A Veterans Service Representative (VSR) will be available to assist you. *If you call, please have this letter with you.* Again, you may contact your Veterans Service Organization, The Disabled American Veterans at 727-319-7444 for assistance.

                            Sincerely yours,

                            TERRY BERUBE
                            Acting Director

                            By Direction of the
                            Under Secretary for Benefits

Ben R. Games, PhD

The Honorable Mel Martinez
Attn: Staff Assistant Marie Tillery
315 E. Robinson St, Landmark Center 1
Orlando, FL 32801

24 December 2005

Ref: Request for phone conversation.

Dear Marie,

I am both pleased and unhappy at the same time. Pleased that you are busy helping veterans and unhappy that there are so many needing help. Sorry about refusing to talk on a machine but I enlisted in the Army 13 August 1942 and was retired from the reserves on the 11 February 1987 without learning to trust them. I was assigned special classified missions for over 27 years of active duty and still believe I served God and Country honorably.

I'm telling you this so that someday when you look back upon your military service you can ask yourself where has the time went. Always remember that everything you do to help a veteran is actually helping yourself. If experience means anything I can assure you that the day will come when you will walk in my shoes.

When you are dealing with an adversary that works under its own rules, laws, and regulations with a staff large enough to eat you alive then you have to stop and think. "If the VA is an aircraft carrier and you are in a row boat needing to slow them down." Would you give up?

The VA is not the enemy but only a big cumbersome organization that wants to deal in percentiles and large numbers. They are in the same league as insurance underwriters and must be treated as such. I'm sure Senator Mel Martinez will explain this better than I can.

Marie remember that "Time Is My Enemy". Senator Martinez offered his assistance in April 2005, and the VA is still refusing to recognize my combat service in Vietnam or active duty 1962-1973. Even if they stall until I fade away don't let them win by default.

For God and Country,

DR. BEN R. GAMES PhD.

A Cry for Help

US Army CRSC Agency
200 Stovall Street
Alexandria, VA 22332-0470   8 January 2006.

REF: Ben R. Games, Major USA Retired. CRSC Claim #91210.

Anyone falling from 800 feet and hitting the ground while in a seated position would have damage to their hips and spine. The veteran reported that the other pilot received a back injury during the combat action but that the troopers who were standing trying to avoid the flames were able to continue fighting. VA records indicate that the Army helicopter came under enemy fire on the approach to LZ Vivian, Vietnam on the 8 November 1969.

The Veterans Administration Medical procedure; Spine Lumbosacral (Min 4 Views). Date & time 02/27/2004 (1042 hrs) show: Reidentified multiple metallic surgical sutures projecting in the midline extending from the lower visualized thoracic spine down to the upper sacrum with many of the sutures broken. Also reindentified status post bilateral total hip arthroplasties.

Interval appearance loss of stature of the L3 vertebral body predominantly with secondary depression of the vertebral endplate. The age is indeterminate. There is a moderate narrowing of the L4-L5 intervertebal disk space and marked narrowing of the L5-S1 intervertebral disk space. There is also multi-level mild lumber spondylosis.

The Traumatic Injuries caused from the crash of a burning helicopter would eventually cause Arthritis and limited motion of limbs with the passage of time. (VA Disability Code 5010 and 5201). VA records indicate that this veteran is a Combat Veteran and the provisions of 38 CFR 3.304 (d) apply.

DR. BEN R. GAMES PhD.

WO1 Mistie Kay Wisniewski
US Army Physical Disability Branch (CRSC)
200 Stovall St
Alexandria, Virginia 22332-0407   16 February 2006

Ref: Phone conversation 14 February 2006.

Dear Mistie,

<u>Medical Records will be mailed to day</u>. A few things you should know.

1. The VA claim is that I never served in Vietnam or on active duty from 1962 to 1973.

2. That I could not have been shot down at LZ Vivian or injured in combat because I wasn't in Vietnam.

3. That I could not have received the DFC, Bronze Star, 13 Air Medals, or Army Commendation Medals because I wasn't in Vietnam.

The VA does admit that I was injured by trauma causing a Hiatal Hernia, ruptured spleen, other internal ruptures, and damage to both hips and back. Both hips were replaced but because I wasn't really in Vietnam the injuries were only a dream so they classified them as NON-COMBAT.

4. The VA has diagnosed me with having Myasthenia Gravis (MG) which is affecting my eyes. I am unable to read paragraphs and believe it or not but any mistakes are truly computer error. According to VA Doctor William Brinkley, MD the disease may have been contacted in Vietnam.

5. The Agent Orange study revealed that I had been exposed to Hepatic "C" from blood transfusions when my spleen was removed or when the VA replaced my hips.

6. VA Doctor James A. Carnahan, MD has told me that I have prostate cancer but not to worry my other injures will cause me to Fad Away before it kills me.

     For God and Country,

                                            DR. BEN R. GAMES PhD.

A Cry for Help

B/G Robert V. Taylor, Assistant AG Army
Department of Military & Veterans Affairs
Michigan Army & Air National Guard
3411 N. Martin Luther King Blvd
Lansing, MI 48906   21 February 2006

Ref: National Guard Files. Games, Ben R. CW-4 #317-18-1165.

Dear Sir,

After CW-4 Cal Stevens retired from the Personnel Office MI Army National Guard I receive a package and a letter. In it was all the MI Army National Guard personnel files pertaining to my military service in the MI ARNG. The letter was about how he thought the files might be confusing to other personnel officers who maybe wouldn't understand but he thought that I would know what to do with the records. At the request of the US Army War College at Carlisle Barracks, Carlisle, Pennsylvania I sent them the files along with the rest of my military records.

I did keep some items that you might find interesting. These are only copies and need not be returned. I can only add that General Schnipke, B/G Radike, your father, (B/G Taylor), and later General Phillips had full knowledge. In fact the day General Schnipke retired your father called to me as I left the headquarters building and asked me to come to the AG office. While your father looked on the Adjutant General said, "Ben I think you have been good for Michigan." I looked at your father, and he was grinning from ear to ear. I didn't really understand as there was never a doubt in my mind.

A few days later I sent $500 in the name of General Schnipke to the Grayling Chapel Fund as I believed then as I do now that a Michigan Civilian Soldier will never stand alone before God or on the battle field.

After I returned from Vietnam I requested assignment to the MI ARNG and while my combat injuries were being repaired the Chief Surgeon a Colonel of the ARNG (forgot his name) and General Phillips would consult with me on the medical procedures proposed by the Air Force doctors. B/G Phillips would fly to Mc Dill AFB, and meet with the Air Force surgeon prior to each operation. It was touch and go for a long time. Then they moved Helen into a room next to the intensive care unit, and read me messages CW-4 Stevens had faxed to the hospital informing them that I was needed in Michigan. With this kind of attention I had to get on my feet fast and six weeks later I made it.

Today I am still fussing with the Veterans Administration about their computer records. I really did served in Vietnam with the 1st Cavalry Division, but this is not what worries me. It's the fact that the VA doesn't believe it, and have made all their medical decisions based upon this strange idea. What if in the next twenty years they deny that the men and women fighting today didn't really go to Iraq?

The US Army Physical Disability Agency (CRSC) 200 Stovall Street, Alexandria, Virginia 22332-0470 WO1 Mistie Kay Wisniewski wrote a note (attached) saying they have no doubts my injuries were result of combat but... When I phoned she said that if I had a General Officer who knew me personally, and would write them on his official letter head confirming I was real they would help.

When I phoned she explained that the person could not be retired. Hell, I'm 82 years old and have had dinner with President Bush, the father not the son and he's retired so they wont accept a letter from him. My options are definitely limited. I am not too smart because I've been recommending that the President ask you to retire and help the VA. It must be I'm too dam old for this. When you see your father again say Hi for me. It all his fault anyway as he should have taught me better.

For God and Country,

DR. BEN R. GAMES PhD.

A Cry for Help

Joseph B. Kelly, CIA Retired
10141 Flagstone Road
Brooksville, FL 34601

352-796-9793

Honorable Ginny Brown Waite, Dist 5
1516 Longworth House Office Bld
Washington D.C., 20515

2 March 2006

Ref: Award of the Purple Heart; Joseph B. Kelly.

Honorable Ginny Brown Waite,

I am presently writing a Vietnamese War historic and biography story, "Confessions of a CIA Interrogator". During my research for the book I came across the records of one of your senior constituents who was wounded while serving the US Army as a civilian in US Army Special Operations commanded by General Abrams. Joseph B. Kelly (Civil Service GS 11) was not only wounded but helped save the lives of many Americans during an attack on the US American Embassy in Ben Tre City, Vietnam.

He did receive "The Medal for Civilian Service in Vietnam (1968-1971)" from General Abrams but not the Purple Heart. It is possible that this award was overlooked and only needs someone who cares about people to bring it to the attention of the right government department.

Joseph Bernard Kelly, (75) born 12 December 1930. Home address; 10141 Flagstone Rd, Brooksville, FL 34602, Phone 352-796-9793.

Attached:
Copy of medical reports on two combat injuries.
Copy of statement of Army Major Barker, Infantry
Copy of The Medal for Civilian Service in Vietnam.
Copy of Criteria for award of the Purple Heart.
SSN available.

If I can be of further assistance I am at your service.

For God and Country,

[signature]

DR. BEN R. GAMES PhD.

Ben R. Games, PhD

Secretary of State
US Department of State
21201 C Street NW
Washington DC 20520   2 March 2006

Ref: Attack on Embassy House, Toy Hoa City, Phu Vien Province, Vietnam

Dear Honorable Condalezza Rice,

No answer required.

I am still trying to prove to the Veterans Administration that I served in Vietnam, but What will be!, Will Be! I did find a report on a combat injury dated 22 September 1970 submitted PYW 50/70 classified Secret and is held in the Nha Trang Region II Hq of the American Embassy. It was not destroyed.

Mr. Joseph Bernard Kelly (GS-11) was wounded by a mortar round hitting the roof over his head. Even though wounded he helped to organize the defense of the Embassy and saved many lives. It is possible that do to the attack being classified secret the Purple Heart was overlooked and not issued.

I do not know the correct procedures or channels for requesting that a Purple Heart be awarded for a civilian wounded while serving his country but only that it is. As the firefight took place on the grounds of the American Embassy 22 September 1970 you may still have an interest in an American who helped when it was needed.

    For God and Country,

Copy: Letter to
Representative Waite,   DR. BEN R. GAMES PhD.
FL Dist #5

A Cry for Help

Joseph B. Kelly, CIA Retired
10141 Flagstone Road
Brooksville, FL 34601

US Army Physical Disability Agency (CRSC)
Attn: WO1, US Army Mistie Kay Wisniewski
Alexandria, Virginia 22332-0470   8 March 2006

Ref: Claim #68021, Major Ben R. Games, Verification Combat Injuries.

Dear WO1 Wisniewski,

I was a CIA Intelligence Officer and Special Police Advisor (5 August 1968 to 2 December 1971) in the Kien Hoa Province in charge of the Dai Phong Program in Vietnam. I worked for Ambassador William Colby.

CWO Ben R. Games (Gentle Ben) was an Aircraft Commander of a CH-47 Chinook helicopter, B Company, 228 Av Bn 1st Cav Div, III Corps Vietnam, and was assigned to support me in moving Province Recon Units (PRU Tiger Scouts) on Snatch and Grab Raids in Vietnam and Cambodia.

He lived in one of our old police trailers on a Thai Firebase called Bearcat. He arrived in Vietnam on the 11 June 1969 and was flown to the Ft Rucker Hospital leaving Vietnam on the 5 February 1970. During this period the DA Form 759 records that he flew 737 combat hours. I personally know that his helicopter was shot down in firefights four (4) times. On the 8 November 1969 the helicopter was on fire when it crashed. He received multi internal ruptures, and was unable to continue. All medical records and missions were classified secret and were forwarded to Nha Trong Region II Hq of the American Embassy.

In the 5 month and 24 days that he was under my control the US Army promoted him from CWO2, to CWO3, and in 1971 to CWO4 and after active duty retirement to Major. The First Cavalry Division awarded him 13 Air Medals, the Bronze Star, and the Distinguished Flying Cross for heroism. He was also awarded a few other medals but not in Vietnam.

Ben asked me to help you. A friend was able to locate a few items that may assist you.

It is possible because the missions and medical records were classified Secret that the award of the Purple Heart was overlooked.

Sincerely,

Ben R. Games, PhD

Channel 8 NBC
8 On Your Side
PO Box #885
Tampa, FL 33601   5 May 2006

Ch; 8 Ph: 813-228-8888

Ref: Cyper-terrorism.

Dear Sirs;

I am a Vietnam Veteran one of the many who have been denied benefits as provided by law.

1. Ben R. Games retired US Army. *** ** 1165. Home Ph: 941-721-6563, 814 Church St Suite 102, Ellenton, FL 34222. (VA Claim C 15 227 804).

2. The government takes $539.00 from my retirement pay each month so the VA can return me the $539.00 as VA compensation. I accept this as it is the law, and the VA need the money.

3. On 31 March 1999 I applied for addition benefits so that I would be guaranteed by law the right to die amongst other veterans. On the 24 Nov 1999 it was refused, and I requested an appeal VA DRO hearing.

4. On the 2 December 2004 I was refused Combat Disability Compensation due to the VA rating that stated that I was never in Vietnam. All my injuries were declared as service connected but Non-Combat by the VA.

5. On the 17 December 2004 I discovered from a VA letter that they were notifying everyone that I was never in combat or in Vietnam and could not have received the Distinguished Flying Cross, Bronze Star, or 13 Air Medals in Vietnam. I again appealed and asked for a VA DRO hearing.

6. The VA has mislead Congresswoman Harris, Senator Martinez, and Senator Nelsen by pretending that they do not know their computer files have been compromised indicating, and that I just want more money.

On the 24 February 2006 I again wrote filing an Appeal and requesting a VA

DRO Hearing. The VA has notified Congresswomen Harris that there are many veterans ahead of me on the waiting list. I accept this as it must be true that the VA Computers records are messed up. It's too bad that our representatives can be ignored or misled by any government department.

I have been on their delay list since March 1999, and the VA can not yet give me a guess of when my name will come up. I am 82 now and time is my enemy. I have requested and received the following VA documents under the freedom of information act.

****

I hereby give Channel 8 and/or 8 On Your Side permission to access and use any of my medical files or military information they may need or require for proving of the statement I have made herein:

I also authorize Channel 8 to use this information.

This may not be in an approved form but I mean it.

****

1. I am attempting to increase my VA disability rating 10% to guarantee my being able to remain with the VA until I die.

2. I am also trying to help the VA correct their records to show that I served in Vietnam and was awarded the DFC for heroism, Bronze Star, and Air Medals.

3. Most of all I would like them to be honest and stop trying to mislead our representatives.

DR. BEN R. GAMES PhD.

Ben R. Games, PhD

WO1 Mistie Kay Wisniewski
US Army Physical Disability Agency (CRSC)
200 Stovall Street
Alexandria, Virginia 22332-0470   19 April 2006

Dear Mistie,

This is a personal letter to thank you for helping me make the decision to continue to toe the line. By now you must have heard or read many thing both bad and good about me. They are more than likely true.

To support your efforts I have appealed the Veterans Administration medical codes based upon their decision that I was not on active duty or served in Vietnam. This should be an easy win but they are using delay tactics and must be hoping I'll fade away so they win by default. My plan is simple. Stay alive and write a historic biography proving what really happened. I will win there is no doubt because it is true.

I did agree to a retirement DD214 so I could accept another assignment. The British Navy helicopter pilots landed us on an island to capture a plane loaded with drugs. The Navy had planned the attack for sundown so it would be at our back and in the eyes of the bad guys. I jumped out leading my native police and charged. By the time we were within the kill zone everyone had outran me and were shooting in every direction. One big bad dude in front of me had a forty-five with a barrel big enough for a cannon ball. I could see the rifling he was so close.

Suddenly there was dead silence. Everyone had ran out a ammunition at the same time. The drug people turned and ran into the brush. My men were all looking at me but I just leaned over sucking in air. We had captured the plane and the drugs but there was no way I was going to chase a bunch of bad dudes in the jungle at night without any ammunition.

Those Navy Pilot looked stunned. They had just witnessed an old man with white hair waving a cane leading a charge of native police in red striped uniforms. The VA doctors were right I'm too dam old, and I'm convinced that the angel guarding the gate into heaven is actually a CW-4 checking to be sure no one gets in before their time.

DR. BEN R. GAMES PhD.

A Cry for Help

Honorable Tom Reynolds
Chairman President's Dinner
300 First St SE
Washington, DC 20003   19 May 2006

Ref: Invitation for President's Dinner Ben R. Games, PhD.

Dear Sir;

It is always an honor to be invited by fellow Republicans to honor our President George W. Bush. My family and friends have supported his father, his brother, and our Commander in Chief with pride and enthusiasm. We will continue to support our President as he leads us in the fight to save America and the world against terrorism.

Unfortunately we live in Congressional District #13 which seems to be on the hit list of the Veterans Administration. This is not the only district that appears to be on their list. Congresswoman Ginny Brown Waite Dist #3 is not talking to her constituents. Her employees use stamp signatures, and the Honorable Mrs. Waite staff assistant has informed me that her office only acts as a forwarding office for other government agencies. Maybe they didn't take the same history courses I did in school, and don't understand what a republic form of government is.

I am presently writing a non-fiction story named "Confessions of a CIA Interrogator", and is based upon the biography of a contract CIA Intelligence Officer. I have located documents that show how he assisted the US Army, and helped save the lives of American Embassy personnel in Vietnam. A copy of the letter to Mrs. Waite is attached.

For the past year I have spend money that I normal donate to Congressional Representatives who assist American Veterans to help the VA correct their computer records. They have denied or do not believe that their computer has been compromised or are covering up the errors for some reason.

We will be unable to attend the dinner. All the money I raise must be used to help our veterans.

                For God and Country;

                                            DR. BEN R. GAMES PhD.

Ben R. Games, PhD

Secretary Veterans Affairs
Mr. James Nicholson
Congressional Office
B-328 Rayburn House Office Building
US House of Representatives
Washington, DC 20515   26 May 2006

Ref: Veterans Computer Compromised. Ben R. Games, PhD,
     VA File# 15 227 804. (1165).

Dear Sir;

The VA Office St Petersburg Region has known about their computer files being compromised for years. A Mr. Terry Berube, Acting Director wrote informing me that the VA had no records of any active duty from 1962 to 1973 or of any Vietnam combat service. My combat injures were changed to service connected with VA Codes 7706, 7346, and 5003. They disregarded my retirement DD214, DFC for heroism, Bronze Star, Air Medal w/13 clusters or the DD Form 759 showing 737 combat hours.

I have been asking for an Appeals Hearing since 1999 and have recently been informed that I'm still on the waiting list but there are many veterans ahead of me.

At my request under the freedom of information act the VA has sent me copies of what records they have found. It included three records that you may find interesting. A copy of a letter from the VA still claiming that I was not in combat dtd 30 November 2005. Also a copy of a VA medical record before their computer was compromised verifying combat, length of service, and Vietnam service dtd 03/01/1998 to 09/20/1999. A copy of a DD214 showing awards and service in Vietnam.

It appears that the VA Computer was compromised by sometime after 1999 who changed the dates of my military service, and then later someone changed the medical records to confirm with the dates in the computer. These changes have caused me to be deprived from benefits provided by law. VA doctors continued medical treatment but informed me about the change. It was suggest that I request an Appeal to correct the records.

                                                DR. BEN R. GAMES PhD.

A Cry for Help

General Peter J. Schoomaker
Chief of Staff, United States Army
1000 Defense, Pentagon
Washington, DC 20301   31 May 2006

Ref: Entitled to the Purple Heart and one Oak Leaf Cluster, Joseph B. Kelly, GS-11 Civilian Employee of MACV Advisor Team #88, Province Officer, Ben Tre City, Kien Hoa Province, Vietnam.

Dear Sir;

As a retired United States Army Soldier, and a believer in the "Army's Freedom Team" I am continually on the watch for anything that is out of the ordinary that reflects badly on our fight against terrorist. I am presently writing a non-fiction adventure story named "Confession of a CIA Interrogator". During my research I located documents that show a USAF T/Sgt Joseph B. Kelly retired after 20 years service and took a position as a civilian GS-11 Army advisor to MACV in Vietnam.

I believe that the Purple Heart award by US War Department General Order 3, of 1932 and currently issued pursuant to Executive Order #12464 dtd 23 February 1984 and Public Law 98-525 dtd 19 October 1984 par "b" sub par (3) that Mr. Joseph B. Kelly may have been overlooked and not issued a Purple Heart for combat injuries received on the 8th June 1970 or when his back was broken during an ambush on Hwy 1 near Tuy Hoa City, Vietnam.

At the time General Creighton Abrams issued him "The Medal for Civilian Service with the Army in Vietnam 1968-1970" the present law was not in affect but every man and woman who puts their lives on the line while serving with US Army, even if they were part of the USAF for 20 years, should be considered as a member of the Army's Freedom Team.

I hereby request that Joseph B. Kelly be accepted as a member of the Army Team and be issued the Purple Heart plus all other awards he is entitled too.

For God and Country,

DR. BEN R. GAMES PhD.

Ben R. Games, PhD

DEPARTMENT OF THE ARMY
OFFICE OF THE DEPUTY CHIEF OF STAFF, G-1
2461 EISENHOWER AVENUE
ALEXANDRIA, VA 22332-0300

REPLY TO
ATTENTION OF

JUN 0 1 2006

Policy and Program Development Division

Honorable Ginny Brown-Waite
United States Representative
20 North Main Street, Suite 200
Brooksville, FL 34601

Dear Congresswoman Brown-Waite:

This is in response to your recent inquiry on behalf of Mr. Joseph B. Kelly, regarding his eligibility for the Purple Heart.

The criteria for the Purple Heart during the time Mr. Kelly was employed in Vietnam required injuries to be directly related to enemy action and were also dependent upon whether the recipient was in direct or indirect combat operations. These determinations were made by commanders and managers at the location of the combat operation. Based on review of the information provided, Mr. Kelly's injury did not meet the criteria for the Purple Heart. The Defense of Freedom Medal was not established at the time of Mr. Kelly's service in Vietnam and may not be presented for an injury prior to its establishment.

Mr. Kelly was an Army civilian employee at the time of his injury and received the Civilian Service in Vietnam Medal for his contributions to the Department of the Army. The support Mr. Kelly provided as a civilian in Vietnam was commendable. Please convey our thanks to him for his service.

Sincerely,

Jeannie A. Davis
Jeannie A. Davis
Chief, Policy and Program Development
Division

A Cry for Help

Department of the Army
Deputy Chief of Staff G-4
2461 Eisenhower Avenue
Alexandria, VA 22332-0300   21 June 2006

Ref: Your Letter dtd 1 June 2006, Policy and Program Division.
To the Honorable Ginny Brown-Waite, 5th District Florida.

Dear Sirs;

I am presently working on a new book titled; "Confession of a CIA Interrogator". It is Non-Fiction and is an adventure story covering a period of 2 & ½ years of the Vietnam War. During research for the book I learned that Mr. Joseph B. Kelly, GS-11, an Army civilian employee was wounded during an attack on the US Embassy at Ben Tre, Vietnam.

Your letter stated that Mr. Kelly did not meet the criteria for the award of the Purple Heart as no commander or manager at the location made any determination of Mr. Kelly's authority to conduct a defense of the Embassy during this combat operation.

I personally interviewed Colonel Geoffrey T. Barker, Retired Infantry, who lead the counter attack and later received the Bronze Star for heroism in this firefight. Mr. Kelly while wounded protected Major General Timmes and organized the defense of the American Embassy.

After the successful repelling of the enemy force Mr. Kelly was treated for his wounds at the MACV Hospital and returned to duty.

I have also located a document that should have been destroyed when the Army left Vietnam which indicates that the attack and firefight for the Embassy was classified secret. This classification may be the reason for denying the award of the Purple Heart but I assure you that when someone is shooting at you the last thing you think of is having to find someone to authorize the defense of Americans. This man heroic actions to save the lives of other Americans should not be forgotten.

           For God and country;

                                      DR. BEN R. GAMES PhD.

Ben R. Games, PhD

Mr Charles A. Vincent, Esq.
310 1st Street SE, Attn: B-2
Washington DC 2003   25 June 2006

Ref:' Conversation and Mr. Ken Mehlman letter dtd 16 June 2006.

Dear Charles,

After our brief conversation and reading of Ken's letter I still think that recognizing all the Vietnam Veterans for their service is only honorable and proper.

Giving them the same recognition as we give those that fought in WW-II, Korean War, and today would get the attention of all service organizations, veterans. and the American people. The award of the Purple Heart to civilians and military personal of the Vietnam war under the same criteria as required for those who served after 1973 would be a good start.

Individual attention from their Congressperson by a phone call or even actually meeting them on a person to person bases would pay big dividends. Just looking into a mirror every morning and reminding themselves that they represent the voters wouldn't hurt.

The citizen soldiers did not lose the war but it was the American people who gave up. Or maybe it was the Communists who spoon fed enough lies to the news media that the politicians gave in. Vietnam was the battle field where the enemy discovered that the American fighting man could not be beaten but by putting a price tag on it the Americans could be told that the Vietnamese people weren't worth fighting to save. Change the dates and it could be today's war against terrorism.

I have written Representative Waite and Congresswoman Harris hoping that they may get to read my letters someday and understand before it is to late.

           For God and Country,

                                                              DR. BEN R. GAMES PhD

A Cry for Help

Commander: PERSCOM
Attn: TAPC-PDO-PA
200 Stovall Street
Alexandria, VA 22332-0471   27 June 2006

Ref: Purple Heart, Ben R. Games, PhD, Major, CW-4, Letter: 20 May06.
   317-18-1165, O-702531, W-2218995, & 19095787.

Dear Sirs;

I am sorry but I may have failed to provide the documentation of the combat medical injuries for the criteria of issuing a Purple Heart. Please find attached a copy of the Combat-Related Special Compensation Division (CRSC) verification.

I also understand that the combat must have been approved and authorized by someone in charge. The impact award of the DFC by the 1st Cavalry Division was awarded 13 Jan 1970 for combat action on 8 November 1969. The combat action at LZ Vivian, Vietnam was approved by the 1st Cavalry Division for the firefight.

The VA statement and claim that I was never in Vietnam or in combat is an error in their computer. At the request of the VA I asked for a correction of Army records and received the attached reply. There is no correction needed for the Army records. The VA Computer had been compromised sometime in the year 2000.

   For God and Country;

                                   [signature]

                                   DR. BEN R. GAMES PhD.

Ben R. Games, PhD

VA Clinic
Dr. James A. Carnahan, MD
4333 N. US Hwy 301
Ellenton, FL 34222   11 July 2006

Ref: Confirmation of Medical Consultation 10 July 2006 for VA File #C15-227-804, Ben R. Games, PhD.

Dear James,

On the 10 July 2006 I was scheduled for a simple medical consultant appointment with you. The purpose was to comply with a request by the Department of the US Army CRSC Agency to determine "How" combat injuries occurred during a firefight at LZ Vivian, Vietnam.

I was informed right upfront that you do not make decisions that have anything to do with VA Compensation. You seemed to believe that I was attempting to get more compensation from the VA. This is far from the truth as there is no monetary gain for me or my family. For every dollar of VA compensation I receive from the VA a dollar is taken from my retirement.

You are a professional who has served in the Vietnam War and from the information I have received are dedicated to those that have served our country. I commend you for your actions in helping veterans who need VA compensation. I too am trying to help the Veterans Administration for they are the backbone of our citizen soldiers. When it was suggested that I should apply for an increase of VA disability I thought it was just a test of the VA system. It is true that if any increase is granted it would only allow that I could die amongst other veterans, but I got your message. I'm going to die anyway so why do I need the VA's help.

I respect your opinions, so I did not show you the copy of a letter from the USAF surgeon who operated on me to repair a large para esophageal hernia caused at the time of the firefight. I have also took your advice about having other VA Doctors review my combat injuries so the computer records can be corrected. I have been notified by phone today that this will be done ASP.

                         For God and Country,

                                                          DR. BEN R. GAMES PhD.

A Cry for Help

Mr. Bill Moor
South Bend Tribune
223 W. Colfax Ave
South Bend, IN 46626

18 July 2006

Dear Bill,

One of my friends read me your article in the South Bend Tribune dtd 11 July 2006. I can now understand why the South Bend Tribune made you one of their staff writers. Not only was it professional written but it made me look good even after my report being 40 years late.

I was told that you sent an E-Mail copy of your article to my E-mail address, but I have problems reading my E-mail. If there is someway I can purchase a copy of the South Bend Tribune for the day that the article appeared I would appreciate a copy.

If there is anything to be learned from a handicap it is only this. You must learn to cope or work around the problem. Never give up and in my case it is a blessing as I can truthfully say that if there is a mistake it is a computer error.

Written but not reread.

For God and Country,

DR. BEN R. GAMES PhD.

Ben R. Games, PhD

Department of the Army
Military Awards Branch
200 Stovall Street
Alexandria, VA 22332-0400   21 July 2006

Ref: LT 7/5/06 Chief, Personnel Services, Purple Heart for Joseph B. Kelly.

Colonel Patrick Devine, Chief, Personnel Services

Dear Colonel Devine;

Reference my letter to General Peter Schoomaker dtd 31 May 2006. Thank you for pointing out the error on the date of the attack on the American Embassy 8 June 1970. The attack started on the night of the 7 June 1970 and continued to the 8 June 1970. Mr. Joseph B. Kelly did not receive medical treatment until 0100 hours on the 8 June 1970 at the MACV Hospital almost two (2) hours after he was wounded. It was during this 2 hour period that he refused medical treatment while helping defend the Embassy. No one can predict what might of happened if he had not continued to resist the enemy.

Then Captain Geoffrey T. Barker who led the counter attack against the enemy was recommended for the Bronze Star with Valor by General Charles Timmes. On the 2nd February 1984, then Major Barker wrote a citation for Mr. Kelly's actions and assistance in the battle. There was one small problem with his citation. Then Major Barker put the date that he was rotated home to the United States on 22 September 1970 as the date of the attack on the Embassy instead of the actual date 7/8 June 1970. See Medical Report of Combat Injury dtd 8 June 1970, Time 0100 hours (am).

US Army Retired, Colonel Geoffrey T. Barker can be contacted by phone #1-727-576-1739 to verify the dates. Colonel Barker is still working for the United States, and this can be verified by direct contact with General Peter J. Schoomaker, US Army Chief of Staff.

I wrote the Honorable Condalezza Rice, US Department of State asking her to verify the attack but I also used the date when Captain Barker returned home instead of the date the attack occurred 7/8 June 1970. The medical report was censored, and the Embassy attack classified "Secret".

DR. BEN R. GAMES PhD

A Cry for Help

Department of Veterans Affairs
Southern Area Office
3322 West End, Suite 408
Nashville, TN 37203   24 July 2006

Ref: Letter Southeastern Director, Mr. Michael Dusenbery, Ben R. Games,
      PhD, C15 227 804 dtd 18 July 2006.

Dear Michael;

Thank you for your informative letter. It is refreshing to know that you are interested in helping to discover what caused the Veterans Computer files to have false information.

I have assisted the VA in medical studies over the years, and when I agreed to test the VA Computer records by using my combat medical records I thought it was only a test. As you know there is no monetary gain for me or my family in any ruling that the Veterans Administration makes. Our country need the VA, and I personally believe that it is the backbone of our citizen soldiers.

If you have truly found a way to protect the VA Computer please notify the Department of Defense, Army Colonel Carl W. Hunt or Mr. Tom Kellerman, Chief Knowledge Officer, Cybrinth. As of January 2006 the USAF was reporting that 80% of all Cyber-terrorism attacks are from foreign sources.

I'm relieved that the VA Computers were not compromised by terrorists, and if I understand you correctly the errors were only caused by VA employees. As you have access to the VA computer, and it has not been compromised then you know that am a retired US Army Major with 70% retirement pay, 30% Combat (CRSC) pay, and 40% VA Disability Pay.

My Bronze Star in Vietnam was from "E" BT 82 Artillery 1st Cavalry Division for action against the enemy not involving flying. The DFC was for heroism during a Firefight at LZ Vivian, Vietnam where I was wounded.

                                              DR. BEN R. GAMES PhD.

Ben R. Games, PhD

DEPARTMENT OF VETERANS AFFAIRS
Veterans Benefits Administration
Washington, D.C. 20420

JUL 0 5 2006

Dr. Ben R. Games
814 Church St.
Ellenton, FL 34222

Dear Dr. Games:

    Your letter to Secretary Nicholson was referred to my office for a response. Your letter indicates that you believe that the VA computer system has been compromised and that you have been waiting for an Appeals Hearing since 1999.

    As Ms. Berube, the then Acting Director of the St. Petersburg Regional Office indicated in her November 30, 2005, letter that office has requested verification of your service from 1962 to 1973. If you have an original or certified copy of your DD214 from that period that would expedite verification, please submit it to the St. Petersburg Regional Office.

    According to VA records, your hearing on May 8, 2006 was canceled. I have spoken with the St. Petersburg Regional Office and they have assured me that they will schedule a new Appeals Hearing for you.

    I hope that this information is helpful to you.

    Sincerely yours,

    Renée L. Szybala, Director
    Compensation and Pension Service

A Cry for Help

General Peter J. Schoomaker
US Army Chief of Staff
1000 Defense, Pentagon
Washington D.C. 20301   1 August 2006

Ref: WO1 Mistie Kay Wisniewski, US Army Combat Special
     Compensation, US Army Physical Disability Agency (CRSC).

Dear Sir;

On the 13 December 2005 I wrote the US Army Physical Disability Agency (CRSC) thanking them for their consideration and told them that they could close the file on my combat injuries received in a firefight at LZ Vivian, Vietnam. I had given up. (Copy of letter attached)

A few weeks later I received a letter from the CRSC asking for more information. Warrant Officer Wisniewski attached a note reminding me that after 81 years I was too old to give up a fight, and that the Army knew of my combat injuries. What she didn't know was that after 22 years with a recommendation for promotion to Lt/Col in the USAF that I had refused to retire. I was accepted in the Army as a CW2, retrained in helicopters, and assigned to the 1st Cavalry Division in Vietnam. Later I retired as a CW4 and after retirement was promoted to Major.

WO1 Wisniewski's note made me realize that I did not have the right to give up. Her professionalism and knowledge of her job is to be commended but most of all her ability to understand that even an old Warrant Officer needs to be reminded once in a while that no soldier stands alone. I have flown in combat alongside of many Warrant Officer Aviators, and I would be proud to have her in the cockpit of my CH-47. She may not be an Army Aviator but she sure thinks like one.

Her ability and support of the CRSC program is a credit to both the US Army, and to all American soldiers. Please convey my personal thanks to WO1 Wisniewski for helping encourage me to toe the line.

                    For God and Country;

                            DR. BEN R. GAMES PhD.

Ben R. Games, PhD

Department Of Veterans Affairs
Regional Office
PO Box 1437
St. Petersburg FL 33731-1437

SEP 2 6 2006

BEN R GAMES
814 CHURCH ST
#102
ELLENTON FL 34222

In reply, refer to:
317/vsc/pre1/jc
File Number: 15 227 804
Ben R. Games

Dear Mr. Games:

We are writing in response to your correspondence dated 12 June 2006, which you submitted to Honorable R. James Nicholson. Your correspondence was forwarded to our office to address your concerns regarding your Veterans Administrations (VA) records.

Regarding your comment in above cited correspondence, "trying to discover when terrorist first got into the VA Computer," VA Compensation and Pension (C&P) electronic records have not been compromised. Your VA medical records are under the jurisdiction of the Veterans Health Administration (VHA). We have not been made aware of VHA records being compromised.

You stated, "Sometime in the year 2000 the computer dates were changed showing...16 years of service, no overseas, no combat, and no DFC, Bronze Star or Air Medals." This change was done in our normal course of business. Documents to substantiate your awards and dates of service, at that time, were not included in your claim file. The documents have since been received and your electronic records updated.

How Can You Contact Us?
If you are looking for general information about benefits and eligibility, you should visit our web site at http://www.va.gov. Otherwise, you can contact us in several ways. Please give us your VA file number, **15 227 804**, when you do contact us.

- Call us at 1-800-827-1000. If you use a Telecommunications Device for the Deaf (TDD), the number is 1-800-829-4833.
- On the Internet at https://iris.va.gov.
- Write to us at the address at the top of this letter.

Sincerely yours,

B. C. Gibbard

B. C. Gibbard
Service Center Manager
cc: VETERANS OF FOREIGN WARS OF THE US

A Cry for Help

Commander; PERSCOM
Attn: TAPC-PDO-PA
200 Stovall Street
Alexander, VA 22332-0471   1 October 2006

Ref: Recommend issue of the PURPLE HEART to Major Ben R. Games, US Army Retired, SSN#317181165, for combat injuries received 8 November 1969 hereinafter referred as; GAMES.

Dear Sirs;

I understand that Senator Mel Martinez's (R) request for issuing a Purple Heart to GAMES for combat injuries was refused because an officer in charge at the time of the firefight did not recommend the award. CW3 Ben R. Games was treated ten hours after the firefight in the USAF Hospital at Phuoc Vinh, and his lung was re-inflated after blood was removed from his chest due to a ruptured spleen. The nature of GAMES combat missions caused his medical reports to be censored, and then sanitized after being forwarded to Nha Trang Region #II, Vietnam.

Major Games is presently receiving 70% military retirement pay for longevity, 60% Combat Disability Pay (CRSC), and 100% VA Disability Compensation. He was placed under my control on the 11 June 1969 and was medi-vac to the Ft Rucker Hospital on 5 February 1970. He supported PRU Tiger Scout operations with aircraft from "E" Bt. Artillery and Company "B", 228th Aviation Battalion, 1st Cavalry Division.

All missions supporting the secret CIA Dai Phong Program were highly classified and sanitized. I hereby certify that all classified military records were officially destroyed as per regulations, and there are no DD Form 759s, written orders, or flight documents, identifying GAMES' assignments in Vietnam or support of the Dai Phong Program. The only AF Forms 5, DA Forms 759, and flight orders available are those that GAMES kept in his personal journal.

I am Joseph B. Kelly, SSN#214267549, former CIA Contract Agent, USAF Retired, Vietnam 1968 to 1971. I was one of four individuals who testified under oath at a Veterans Administration, St Petersburg Region hearing on the VA Computer being compromised by someone unknown. Testimony was taken and recorded on the 23 August 2006 at the VA Regional Offices, St Petersburg, Florida. A transcript of the testimony is available from the Veterans Administration.

I was also a CIA Intelligence Officer and Special Police Advisor (5 August 1968 to 2 December 1971) in Kien Hoa Province working in the secret CIA Dai Phong Program in Vietnam. I worked directly for Mr. William Colby, CIA. GAMES, a member of the 1st Cavalry Division, was one of my assets. He assisted my missions by flying PRU Tiger Scouts in Snatch and Grab Raids in Vietnam and Cambodia.

During the VA hearing I learned that GAMES had never received the Purple Heart recognizing the combat injuries he received during a firefight at LZ Vivian, Vietnam. This was not a surprise as I was injured in enemy ambushes twice in Vietnam, and because of the classification of the work my medical reports were also censored so No Purple Hearts was issued.

I first met GAMES during 1948 in Okinawa while he was helping prepare for the Chinese Government's move from China to Taiwan in 1949. GAMES is a highly trained specialist in this type of work and is also a Nuclear Weapons Officer, Electronic Engineer, Fire Control Officer, Accountant, USAF Senior Pilot, and a US Army Senior Aviator.

Mr. Bill Colby, CIA and the Commanding General of Special Operations knew of GAMES' successes in 1966/67 in Vietnam. During 1968 GAMES was sent to Ft Rucker and trained in all types of Army helicopters. With the cooperation of the 1st Cavalry Division Commanding General GAMES was reassigned to Vietnam in support of Special Operation assignments. GAMES would fly Company "B" helicopters on normal Cavalry missions so he would always be within a few minutes of any location where support was needed. After GAMES was released from any special mission he would go back to flying Company "B" lifts. GAMES never carried more that 45 American Troops but many times he had over 100 packs counting the PRU Scouts aboard the Chinook helicopter.

GAMES was qualified in all Army aircraft and helicopters in Vietnam. During his assignment as one of my assets he had his CH-47 helicopter shot down four times by enemy fire. On the day he was wounded by enemy fire he was flying under DNIF orders. GAMES had been grounded on the 7

A Cry for Help

November 1969 for having flown over 120 combat hours during the past 30 days.

Do to a shortage of Aircraft Commanders the "B" Company Commander ordered all instructor pilots to give Aircraft Commander's flight check outs. GAMES was shot down in flames and both pilots received the DFC for heroism and the crew were each awarded an Air Medal. GAMES was cleared to fly on the 9th November 1969 after his lung was reinflated. He remained under my operational control but was never able to fly alone again. After many visits to the hospital and after receiving four units of whole blood it was decided he needed operations that could not be performed in Vietnam.

President John F. Kennedy signed an Executive Order on 25 April 1962 stating now and hereafter that any military or civilian serving in any capacity with an Armed Force and being wounded would receive the Purple Heart. President Ronald Reagan's Executive Order 12464 dtd 23 February 1984 and Public Law 98-525, 19 October 1984 reinforced the law including injuries from acts of terrorism. In 1998 it was changed again removing the award to civilians who were injured by an enemy attack after 1998.

GAMES was flying for the 1st Cavalry Division at the time of the ambush and was awarded the DFC for heroism and 13 Air Medals. I assumed the Army would recognize his injuries and recommend issuing a Purple Heart. This was not done, and he was returned to the United States by Saigon Special Operations. GAMES was awarded 60% Combat Disability Pay (CRSC), and 100% VA compensation but because of his sanitized medical records the Veterans Administration had no record of his Vietnam service..

        Sincerely Yours,

                Joseph B. Kelly, former CIA Contract Officer
                10141 Flagstone Rd.
                Brooksville, FL 34601

Copy to: Senator
Mel Martinez   Ph 352-796-9793
Ben R. Games, PhD

Ben R. Games, PhD

DEPARTMENT OF VETERANS AFFAIRS
VA Regional Office
P.O. Box 1437
St. Petersburg, FL 33731

Ben R. Games

VA File Number
15 227 804

Represented by:
VETERANS OF FOREIGN WARS OF THE US

Decision Review Officer Decision
October 3, 2006

INTRODUCTION

The records reflect that you are a veteran of the World War II Era, Korean Conflict Era, Vietnam Era and Peacetime. You served in the Air Force from November 23, 1942 to November 10, 1947, from May 30, 1948 to September 30, 1962, from May 30, 1948 to December 5, 1953 and from July 2, 1973 to December 31, 1977. Separation Document (DD 214) dated May 2, 1970 from the Army / Army National Guard shows the veteran service in Vietnam during the period Jun 11, 1969 to February 5 1970. We received a Notice of Disagreement from you on February 18, 2005 about one or more of our earlier decisions. Based on a review of the evidence listed below, we have made the following decision(s) on your claim.

DECISION

1. Entitlement to individual unemployability is granted effective March 15, 2004.

2. Evaluation of postoperative bilateral inguinal hernia, post operative gall bladder and post operative hiatal hernia and status post two gastric ulcers with recurrent anemia,

which is currently 10 percent disabling, is increased to 40 percent effective March 15, 2004.

3. Evaluation of spontaneous pneumothorax, residuals, which is currently 0 percent disabling, is increased to 10 percent effective March 15, 2004.

4. Basic eligibility to Dependents' Educational Assistance is established from March 15, 2004.

EVIDENCE

- VA examination conducted by the James A. Haley Veterans Hospital of Tampa FL dated November 13, 2004
- Newspaper article regarding the veteran dated July 20, 2006
- Letter from the veteran dated July 26, 2006
- The evidence of record has been reviewed and considered.
- Treatment records from the James A Haley Veterans Hospital of Tampa FL for the period March 21, 1996 to October 1, 2006, regarding myasthenia gravis.
- Treatment records from the James A Haley Veterans Hospital of Tampa FL for the period March 21, 1996 to October 1, 2006, regarding hip replacements.
- Transcript of Decision Review Officer Hearing dated August 23, 2006
- Binder of documents presented at hearing by the veteran, aproximately 100 pages

REASONS FOR DECISION

1. Entitlement to individual unemployability.

Entitlement to individual unemployability is granted because the claimant is unable to secure or follow a substantially gainful occupation as a result of service-connected disabilities.

Entitlement to Individual Unemployability includes consideration of all service-connected disabilities and those granted under 38 USC 1151.

A 30 percent evaluation is assigned for splenectomy. An evaluation of 30 percent is assigned for residuals of a splenectomy.

A 40 percent evaluation is assigned for postoperative bilateral inguinal hernia, postoperative gall bladder and postoperative hiatal hernia and status post two gastric ulcers with recurrent anemia. An evaluation of 40 percent is granted if the record shows intercurrent episodes of abdominal pain at least once a month partially or completely relieved by ulcer therapy, with mild and transient episodes of vomiting or melena.

Ben R. Games, PhD

Statement of the Case	Department of Veterans Affairs St. Petersburg Regional Office		Page 49 10/03/2006
NAME OF VETERAN Ben R. Games	VA FILE NUMBER 15 227 804	SOCIAL SECURITY NR 317 181 165	POA VETERANS OF FOREIGN WARS OF THE US

DE NOVO REVIEW

This review was made by a Veterans Administration Officer on the 23 August 2006. Four witnesses testified under oath concerning the military fire fight at LZ Vivian on the 8th November 1969. A transcript of the interrogations is available at the VA St Petersburg Regional Office.

This is a true copy of the findings made by the VA concerning the veterans combat injuries received during one firefight with a enemy of the United States. There are 9 pages in the VA Decision Letter dated the 3 October 2006, and 66 pages in the DE NOVO REVIW.

REASONS AND BASES:

De Novo Review conducted by Decision Review Officer

It is the determination of the Decision Review Officer that the evidence of record did support a change in the determination as provided in Rating Decision dated December 17, 2004. This decision is based on a De Novo review of the evidence contained in the claims record without deference to the prior determination under authority of 38 CFR 3.2600.

The evidence of record, specifically a Separation Document (DD 214) dated May 2, 1970 from the Army / Army National Guard shows the veteran service in Vietnam during the period Jun 11, 1969 to February 5 1970. Therefore the veteran's service on Active Duty in the Republic of Vietnam is established.

The evidence of record shows the veteran's awards include the following: Bronze Star Medal for meritorious service in connection with military operation against a hostile force in the Republic of Vietnam (circa June 1969 to February 1970), Air Medal for meritorious achievement while participating in aerial flight in the Republic of Vietnam, (circa June 1969 to February 1970), The Distinguished Flying Cross for heroism while participating in aerial flight (November 8 1969). The basis for the award was that on approach to the landing zone the aircraft was struck by enemy fire, which caused both engines to fail and ignited a fire. Based upon this evidence the veteran is a Combat Veteran and the provisions of 38 CFR 3.304 (d) apply.

A Cry for Help

Commander: PERSCOM
Attn: TAPC-PDO-PA
200 Stovall Street
Alexandria, VA 22332-0471   20 October 2006

Ref: Military Awards, Purple Heart, Par 2-8 AR 600-8-22. Ben R. Games, PhD, Major, 317-18-1165.

Dear Sirs;

As per Executive Order signed by President John F. Kennedy on the 25 April 1962, and Executive Order #12464 dtd 23 February 1984 and Public Law 98-525, 19 October 1984 par "b" sub par (1) the undersigned is entitled for the decoration of the Purple Heart.

>CW-3 Ben R. Games ***-**-1165
>Aircraft Commander, CH-47 Chinook Helicopter
>CO B, 228th Avn. Bn. 1st Cavalry Division
>Bearcaat, Vietnam
>
>Firefight at LZ Vivian, 8 November 1969

Copies of awards for the DFC for heroism, Bronze Star, and 13 Air Medals.

Copy of DA Form 759, DD214, and after action combat photos are attached.

Injures form enemy fire on the 8 November 1969 resulted in a cracked rib, a collapsed lung with an hiatal hernia, a ruptured spleen, and damaged hips resulting in both being replaced. Fluid was drained from the lung and chest by a surgeon at the Phouc Vinh USAF Hospital on the 9th November 1969. The lung inflated itself and no hospitalization was ordered.

Entered combat 11 Jun 1969, flew 737 combat hours, medi-vac to Ft Rucker Hospital 5 Feb 1970.

The undersigned is a retired US Army Major with 70% active duty retirement pay, 60% Combat Disability (CRSC) pay, and 100% VA Disability Compensation.

>DR. BEN R. GAMES PhD.

Ben R. Games, PhD

Honorable Senator Mel Martinez
US Senator, Florida
Senate Office Building
Washington D.C. 20510

1 November 2006

Ref: Your actions delaying President Bush visit to Hanoi, Vietnam.

Dear Mel,

I believe that your actions are more important than your staff or associates can ever guess. Anything you can do to save our President from the biggest mistake of his Presidency will someday be recorded as a brilliant and courageous action of a patriot.

I have read about your attempts to withhold your committees approval of the President's visit to Hanoi until the Communist Vietnamese Government releases a Vietnamese American Citizen. It's a brilliant move but I will predict that they will release her right after this months elections are over unless torture during interrogation has left her disfigured, and then she will join other American MIA.

The Communists need the president's visit to bolster their choice of candidate's chances in the next presidential elections. You can verify what I've written by asking Senator John McCain how prisoners are interrogated by the Vietnamese, or Senator John Kerry about financial investing in Vietnam. Remember that the Communist anti-Christ peace sign was changed to the dollar sign to support the terrorist attacking Americans today.

For God and Country,

DR. BEN R. GAMES PhD.

A Cry for Help

Commander; PERSCOM
Attn: TAPC-PDO-PA
200 Stovall Street
Alexander, VA 22332-0471   1 November 2006

Ref: Issue of the PURPLE HEART to Major Ben R. Games, US Army Retired, SSN#317181165, for combat injuries received 8 November 1969. De Novo Review conducted by a VA Decision Review Officer dtd 10/03/06.

Dear Sirs;

CW3 Ben R. Games was treated ten hours after the firefight at LZ Vivian in the USAF Hospital at Phuoc Vinh, and his lung was re-inflated after blood was removed from his chest due to a ruptured spleen. The nature of GAMES combat missions caused his medical reports to be censored.

Major Games is presently receiving 70% military retirement pay for longevity, 30% Combat Disability Pay (CRSC), and 70% VA Disability Compensation. He was placed under my control on the 11 June 1969 and was flown to the Ft Rucker Hospital on 5 February 1970. He supported PRU Tiger Scout operations with Army aircraft from "E" Bt. Artillery and Company "B", 228th Aviation Battalion, 1st Cavalry Division.

All missions supporting the secret CIA Dai Phong Program were highly classified and sanitized. I hereby certify that all classified military and medical records were officially destroyed as per regulations, and there are no DD Form 759s, written orders, or flight documents, identifying GAMES' assignments in Vietnam or support of the Dai Phong Program. The only AF Forms 5, DA Forms 759, and flight orders available are those that GAMES may have in his personal journal.

I am Joseph B. Kelly, SSN#214267549, former CIA Contract Agent, USAF Retired, Vietnam 1968 to 1971. I was one of four individuals who testified under oath at a VA St Petersburg Region hearing on the VA Computer being compromised by someone unknown. Testimony was taken and recorded on the 23 August 2006 at the VA Regional Offices, St Petersburg, Florida.

I was also a CIA Contract Intelligence Officer and Special Police Advisor (5 August 1968 to 2 December 1971) in Kien Hoa Province working in the secret CIA Dai Phong Program in Vietnam. I worked directly for Mr. William Colby, CIA. GAMES, a member of the 1st Cavalry Division, was one of my assets. He assisted my missions by flying PRU Tiger Scouts in Snatch and Grab Raids in Vietnam and Cambodia.

During the VA hearing I learned that GAMES had never received the Purple Heart recognizing the combat injuries he received during a firefight at LZ Vivian, Vietnam. This was not a surprise as I was injured in enemy ambushes twice in Vietnam, and because of the classification of the work my medical reports were also censored so No Purple Hearts was issued.

I first met GAMES and his wife Helen during 1948 in Okinawa while he was helping prepare for the Chinese Government's move from China to Taiwan (Formosa) in 1949. GAMES is a highly trained specialist in this type of work and is also a Nuclear Weapons Officer, Electronic Engineer, Fire Control Officer, Accountant, USAF, and a US Army Senior Aviator. In Vietnam they lived on a Thai Firebase named Bear Cat. Their bodyguards were a infantry company of Thai soldiers. The South Vietnamese government contact and friend was Mr. Cat Lee, Minister of Information. The Korean Military Attaché also assigned an Intelligence Officer to assist GAMES on missions with the Korean Marine Whitehorse Division.

Mr. Bill Colby, CIA and the Commanding General of Special Operations knew of GAMES' successes in 1966/67 in Vietnam. During 1968 GAMES was sent to Ft Rucker and trained in all types of Army helicopters. With the cooperation of the 1st Cavalry Division Commanding General GAMES was assigned to Vietnam in support of Special Operation assignments. GAMES would fly Company "B" helicopters on normal Cavalry missions so he would always be within a few minutes of any location where support was needed. After GAMES was released from any special mission he would go back to flying Company "B" lifts. GAMES never carried more that 45 American Troops but many times he had over 100 packs counting the PRU Scouts aboard the Chinook helicopter.

GAMES was qualified in all Army aircraft and helicopters in Vietnam. During his assignment as one of my assets he had his CH-47 helicopter shot down four times by enemy fire. On the day he was wounded by enemy fire he was flying under DNIF orders. GAMES had been grounded on the 7 Nov. 1969 for having flown over 120 combat hours during the past 30 days.

Do to a shortage of Aircraft Commanders the "B" Company Commander ordered all instructor pilots to give Aircraft Commander's flight check-outs. GAMES was shot down in flames and both pilots received the DFC for heroism and the crew were each awarded an Air Medal. GAMES was cleared to fly on the 9th November 1969 after his lung was re-inflated. He remained under my operational control but was never able to fly alone again. After many visits to the hospital and after receiving four units of whole blood it was decided he needed operations that could not be performed in Vietnam.

President John F. Kennedy signed an Executive Order on 25 April 1962 stating now and hereafter that any military or civilian serving in any capacity with an Armed Force and being wounded would receive the Purple Heart. President Ronald Reagan's Executive Order 12464 dtd 23 February 1984 and Public Law 98-525, 19 October 1984 reinforced the law including injuries from acts of terrorism. In 1998 it was changed again removing the award to civilians who were injured by an enemy attack after 1998.

GAMES was flying for the 1st Cavalry Division at the time of the ambush and was awarded the DFC for heroism and 13 Air Medals. I assumed the Army would recognize his injuries and recommend issuing a Purple Heart. This was not done, and he was returned to the United States by Saigon Special Operations. Because of his sanitized military and medical records the Veterans Administration had ruled that he was never Vietnam or in combat.

        Sincerely Yours,

                Joseph B. Kelly, former CIA Contract Officer
                10141 Flagstone Rd.
                Brooksville, FL 34601

Copy to: Ph 352-796-9793
Ben R. Games, PhD

Ben R. Games, PhD

Honorable John McCain
US Senator
Senate Office Building
Washington DC, 20510

3 November 2006

Ref: Senator Mel Martinez attempt to save a United States citizen from Communist Vietnamese interrogation.

Dear Veteran,

Please speak to Senator Martinez and offer your support even it is only to let him know what torture the woman is going through. Some may say that she is only a Vietnamese woman who is working against the Communist but that is not a crime even in the United States. As long as she is a citizen of our great nation she must not stand alone.

I'm sorry about writing emotionally but the American Ambassador in Vietnam during the war was an ass and even classified attacks on the Embassy in Ben Tre City 8th June 1970 as secret to prevent the American people from learning that the Paris Pease Talks where actually the Paris Pease Accord dictating terms of our turning over the Vietnamese people to the Communists. You see I can't even write the word surrender.

If you are too busy to phone him maybe you could mail him your book and send me the bill. I will be glad to pay for it.

For God and Country,

Enclosed;
Copy of letter to
Senator Martinez.

DR. BEN R. GAMES PhD.

A Cry for Help

Ms Barbara Routen
Staff Correspondent
The Tampa Tribune
505 W. Robertson St.
Brandon, FL 33511

16 November 2006

Ref: VHPA story dtd 11 November 2006.

Dear Barbara,

Thank you for honoring me by sending a copy of your excellent story. The reunion at the Hillsborough County Veterans Park of combat helicopter pilots who fought in the Vietnam War should be of great interest to everyone. Your news article gave me great pleasure.

I've read in the Tampa Tribune that today less than 1% of American citizens are veterans who have served our great nation. If this is true then the freedoms we enjoy today are based on what these few men and women have given us. The only thing I regret is that today I'm too dam old to fly a Army Cobra. At 82 I'll continue fighting to protect America, even if someone has to help me toe the line.

Thank everyone at the Tampa Tribune for helping tell the story of how our citizen-soldiers are helping to keep the Dark Force terrorists from Florida. It is too bad that the people of Florida passed an Amendment to our Florida Constitution not to recognize Florida resident military veterans over the age of 65 unless they enlisted while a resident of Florida. I wander how many VHPA Veterans at the reunion actually joined the military services from the state of Florida?

For God and Country,

DR. BEN R. GAMES PhD.

Ben R. Games, PhD

DEPARTMENT OF THE ARMY
ARMY REVIEW BOARDS AGENCY
1901 SOUTH BELL STREET
ARLINGTON VA 22202-4508

February 8, 2007

Case Management Division/sra
GAMES, BEN R.
AR20080002197

MAJ Ben R. Games (Retired)
814 Church St # 102
Ellenton, FL 34222-2318

Dear Major Games:

    On behalf of the Army Board for Correction of Military Records (ABCMR) to which this office provides administrative support, we acknowledge receipt of your request for reconsideration dated January 18, 2008. Your application has been assigned the case number shown above.

    Much time is involved in obtaining military records and staffing applications. There is a large volume of applications pending before the ABCMR and in fairness to all the ABCMR acts on applications according to the dates they are received. It takes approximately 10 months from the time an application is received until all actions are completed.

    If your address changes during this time, please notify us at the address above. Reference your case number and provide your new address so we may maintain contact with you.

    Thank you for patience as we obtain your records and consider your application.

Sincerely,

Walter Avery
Chief, Case Management Division

A Cry for Help

Army Review Board Agency
Mr. Walter Avery, Chief
Case Management Division
1901 South Bell Street
Arlington, VA 22202-4508

15 February 2008

Ref: Case Number AR20080002197, Games, Ben R.; PhD, Maj, CW4.

Dear Mr. Avery;

Thank you for the letter assigning a Case Number to my request. I have been sending different Thesis written for the USAF University, US Army War College, and Carlisle Barracks along with 126 pages of medical records in support of the request for correction of ABCMR's report.

The Veterans Administration spent years researching my medical records before they realized mine wasn't a normal soldier's life. The VA military medical records cover a period of 44 years 4 month, 28 days of military service and are over a 1000 pages.

Mr. Kenneth A. Thie, Director VFW Service Office, PO Box 1437 (Rm 217A) has copies of some of the actual DD Form 759 and USAF Form 5's. The military orders of some of my assignments during WWII are at the Army War College and others are at the USAF Air University. Some are classified. I am aware that some of the records have been sanitized or rebuilt to support new assignments. The requested for the Purple Heart was made when I learned that the men who were killed or wounded serving with me including myself were not on the official Vietnam Casualty List.

I have already sent the following Theses: The Bangkok Drop, A Terrorist Mirror, VFW Biography of Games by Vicki Lopez, Army Correction of Records; Rebuttal, and referred to research for books "Confession of a CIA Interrogator" (2007) "Jihad Vietnam" (2008). If any of these have been lost please notify me. I will replace them.

Written but not reread.

MAJ Ben R. Games, Ph.D., USAF (Ret.)
814 CHURCH ST # 102
ELLENTON, FL 34222-2318

Ben R. Games, PhD

Army Review Board Agency
Chief, Congressional and Special Actions
Mr. Rick A. Schweigert
1901 South Bell St, 2nd Floor
Arlington, VA 22202-4508

4 February 2008

Ref: Q20080000318, Major Ben R. Games, PhD, CW4, TCNA-6.

Dear Mr. Schweigert;

I received your letter today concerning my appeal of the ABCMR Denial of corrections as listed on DD Form 149. It appears that if you are receiving 15,000 thousand Appeal requests per year then Command should be made aware of the mistakes being made by personnel clerks. I would have thought that it should be under a 100 for the entire Army.

When I learned that soldiers in the body bags my helicopter delivered to the Saigon Mortuary Pad were not counted as historically casualties it upset me. I didn't keep the names of the Americans wounded or KIA on classified missions, and I sure didn't know there was an official Vietnam Casualty List. My request for the Purple Heart was suggested in a letter from the VA, and is in the hope that anyone who was wounded while flying with me could use the information to help prove that they were in a real firefight.

Actually there is no hurry about my appeal. I didn't serve America for the medals. My VA doctor has informed me that I am on the launch pad for my next assignment but couldn't tell me when, only that it was sooner than later. I do have a personal request: Please contact the Director Kenneth A. Thie, of the VFW Service Office, Department of Florida, PO Box Office 1437 (Rm 217A), St Petersburg, FL 33731 if I die before you correct the records. The VFW has copies of the actual DD Form 759's and can use your findings to help other Veterans who flew with me.

Copy to: Mr. Thie

For God and Country;

MAJ Ben R. Games, Ph.D., USAF (Ret.)
814 CHURCH ST # 102
ELLENTON, FL 34222-2318

A Cry for Help

Feb 2007

RECEIPT AND ACKNOWLEDGMENT

The undersigned JOSEPH B. KELLY, of 10141 Flagstone Road, Brooksville, Florida 34602, hereby acknowledge the following:

    A.   I furnished to Ben R. Games, Ph.D, the documents described immediately below for his use as reference material for his book "Confession of a CIA Interrogator":

1. Article from "The Drop" Special Forces magazine.
2. Hand written notes and pictures of Woody Hays, Ohio State.
3. Drawings of PRU Compounds and cities of Toy, Hoa and Plieku.
4. Notes on CIA interrogations and pictures.
5. Hand written notes on name of prisoners interrogated.
6. Hand written notes on meetings with Bill Colby, head of CIA operations in Vietnam.
7. Copy of newspaper clippings on medals awarded by the South Vietnamese Government.
8. Hand written notes on using Navy Swift Boats on the Mekong River and from Army helicopters to assist in the capture of Viet Cong.
9. Copy of letters from Capt. Geoffrey T. Barker giving credit for Joe Kelly, as the originator of the Secret CIA Dai Phong Program.
10. Hand written notes on firefights and capturing prisoners to interrogate, and attacks on the Tiger Scouts PRU Compound.
11. Copy of Statistical Report on elimination of 112 enemy September 69 to February 70.
12. Copy of memo from Mr. Gage McAfte, CIA Legal Affairs.
13. Hand written notes on helping Vietnamese children.
14. Hand written notes on assignments to destroy Viet Cong cells in cities along the North Vietnamese Army transportation routes to Saigon.
15. Copy of letters from Ken Tolliver, CIA Jeweler.
16. Notes on death of an American Army Captain.
17. Notes on the one-way bridge and use of asset Army CW3 Games.
18. Hand written notes on snatch and grab missions.
19. Copy of letters and instructions.
20. Copy of Hanoi Jane's Apology "The Washington Times".
21. Medical Reports classified Secrets concerning injuries received by Joe Kelly in ambushes of the enemy.
22. Hand written notes on CIA plane crash at Kien Pheng.

    B.   I allowed Dr. Games to have access to certain photographs and other documents, not listed above, that were reviewed in my office in Brooksville, Florida and never removed from that office by Dr. Games.

    C.   I have received each and every document listed in Item A, above, back from Dr. Games, who has assured me he has kept no copies of any part thereof.

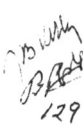

153

Ben R. Games, PhD

D. As Dr. Games finished each chapter of his book, it was sent to me for review. I reviewed and edited the content of each chapter for correctness of content and historical accuracy prior to the book being submitted by Dr. Games to the publisher.

E. From my review and editing of the transcript of Dr. Games for the book "Confession of a CIA Interrogator" the story portrayed therein is an accurate description of the events depicted in the book, and my verification is based upon my experience as a CIA contract agent in Southeast Asia during the applicable time period.

IN WITNESS WHEREOF, I have signed this document the ___3___ day of ___Feb___ _____, 2007.

Joseph B. Kelly
JOSEPH B. KELLY

STATE OF FLOIRDA } S/S
COUNTY OF __MANATEE__ }

I HEREBY CERTIFY that, on this day, personally appeared before me, an officer duly authorized to administer oaths and take acknowledgments, JOSEPH B. KELLY, personally known by me (or, if not personally known by me, who produced the following proof of identification __Military ID__), and acknowledged before me that the foregoing instrument was executed freely and voluntarily for the purposes therein expressed.

WITNESS my hand and official seal at __Ellenton__, County of __Manatee__, _____, and State of Florida, this __3rd__ day of __February__, 2007.

Mary Ann Englert
NOTARY PUBLIC State of Florida at Large

Print Name: __Mary Ann Englert__

MARY ANN ENGLERT
MY COMMISSION # DD 463909
EXPIRES: August 21, 2009
Bonded Thru Notary Public Underwriters

A Cry for Help

DEPARTMENT OF THE ARMY
UNITED STATES ARMY WAR COLLEGE AND CARLISLE BARRACKS
CARLISLE, PENNSYLVANIA 17013-5021

VFW

We'd do anything for this country!

REPLY TO
ATTENTION OF

February 12, 2007

U.S. Army Heritage and Education Center
ATTN: Collection Management
950 Soldiers Drive
Carlisle, Pennsylvania 17013-5021

Telephone: 717-245-3094
E-mail: Greg.Statler@carlisle.army.mil

Maj. Ben R. Games, USAF, (Ret.)
814 Church Street
Suite 102
Ellenton, FL 34222-2318

Dear Maj. Games:

    On behalf of the U.S. Army Heritage and Education Center, thank you for your unconditional donation of your book, Confession of a CIA Interrogator. You have enriched our collection by your generosity.

    The purpose of this letter is to acknowledge that your materials have been received. If you have any questions regarding this, please contact us at anytime.

    Thank you again for your contribution. Your support of the Center and its mission of telling the Army's story is greatly appreciated.

Sincerely,

Gregory E. Statler
Registrar

Ben R. Games, PhD

Kenneth O. Preston, Sergeant Major of the Army
Department of the Army
Washington DC 20310-0200   12 March 2007

Ref: Censorship

Dear Sergeant Major,

I am the author of a nonfiction book "Confession of a CIA Interrogator". It is about the work of a CIA Contract Agent during 2 ½ years of the Vietnam War. At the time I was an Army CW3 Aviator in the 1st Cavalry Division and flew special operation missions with Province Recon Units (PRU) until I was returned home due to combat injuries.

About six months ago I answered a letter from General Peter J. Schoomaker, Chief of Staff which was opened and stamped by the mailroom in the Pentagon. The letter was marked return to sender. I took the letter to the US Post Office and allowed them to read the letter as it was a pledge to support the US Army. The Postal Inspector took the letter and said they would try to deliver it, but could not force the Pentagon Mailroom to do anything. This time it never came back.

Today I receive another letter signed by yourself, General Schoomaker, and Secretary of the Army Francis Harvey asking for a reply to the ARMY Relief Fund. I intend to reply and send a donation but maybe I'm on a list of persons who's mail gets lost. I'm going to enclose a fifty dollar check donation so I can tell if the letter gets past the mailroom.

Senator Martinez told me that they were going to pass a law where anyone claiming an award would have to prove they had it or face prison. It sounds like a good law but how about the three Navy Seals who were awarded the Medal of Honor where their names are even classified secret. Last month Lt/Col Sylvia A. Bennett, Chief of the awards branch wrote and informed me that the soldiers who's bodies I delivered to the Saigon Mortuary pad were not historically a casualty of the Vietnam War.

For God and Country,

DR. BEN R. GAMES PhD.

A Cry for Help

Honorable Vern Buchanan
Congressman 13 District FL
House Office Building
Washington D.C., 20515-0913   28 March 2007

Ref: Your letter dtd 14 March 2007 to Ben R. Games, PhD.

Dear Vern,

There is no need to bother Joni as I have no personal need for assistance. I was only trying to assist in your next election by speaking of a subject that everyone could support. Well not everyone as I'm sure Muslims and Communists are not on your team. Two years is actually a very short time before the next election and campaigning can not start to soon.

The idea of awarding everyone killed or injured in the Vietnam War a Purple Heart even though they were not historically counted as a casualty was not mine. Miss Marie Tillery of Senator Martinez staff suggested that the use of military secrecy for political reasons was an insult to all veterans. I phoned your office but no one I talked with understood the need to take up a cause that would help both Republican and Democrats.

Basically it would involve the recognition and support of President John F. Kennedy's Executive Order on the 25th April 1962 extending eligibility for the Purple Heart to any military or civilian national who while serving under competent authority in any capacity with any armed force…has been or may hereafter be wounded. Also President Ronald Reagan signed an Executive Order #123464 on the 23rd February 1984 to include all those wounded or killed as a result of a terrorist attack. It also stated that the award was not by recommendation but only that the individual met the criteria of being wounded and received medical treatment.

During the VFW Political Action Committee meeting in Sarasota during your last campaign I met your staff and was very impressed. I can find no fault with success, and I wish you well.

               For God and Country,

                                  DR. BEN R. GAMES PhD.

Ben R. Games, PhD

Department of the Army
US Army Human Resource Command
Military Awards Branch, Chief Lt/Col Sylvia A. Bennett
200 Stovall Street, Alexandria, VA 22332-0400   12 April 2007

Ref: Your letter dated 6 March 2007, Ben R. Games, PhD, Major.

Dear Lt/Col Bennett,

Please find attached a copy of the DD Form 149. The form was submitted direct to the Army Review Agency Support Division, St Louis, MO.

Paragraph two of your letter does not seem to meet the criteria of President John F. Kennedy's Executive Order issued on the 25 April 1962. The order extended eligibility for the Purple Heart to be awarded to all military personal and to any civilian national of the United States serving under competent authority in any capacity with an armed force ... has been or may hereafter be wounded. This order has not been rescinded, and President Ronald Reagan's Executive Order #12464, 23 February 1984, also included military and civilians wounded or killed as a result of a terrorist attack.

My Army Combat-Related Special Compensation Division (CRSC) rating is 60%, and the VA is 100% Disability with 70% combat related. The VA Decision Letter dated 3 October 2006 and De Novo Review state that the veteran was shot, suffered a lung collapse, and underwent surgery. The bases for the Distinguished Flying Cross for heroism award was that on the approach to a LZ in Vietnam the helicopter was struck by enemy fire which caused both engines to fail and ignited a fire. Based on this evidence the VA ruled that I am a Combat Veteran and the provisions of 38 CFR 3.304 (d) apply.

For God and Country,

DR. BEN R. GAMES PhD.

A Cry for Help

Mrs. Laura Bush
The White House
Washington D.C. 20500

17 April 2007

Dear Mrs. Bush,

I have always wandered if you received the book "Santa's Secret" that I sent you two years ago. Being a citizen soldier and not a famous writer may have caused someone to forget to let you read it. During my daydreams I imagine that it must have been so good that someone took it home for their children.

The story was a true experience for the children of the Turks and Caicos Islands, and I enjoyed writing about how Father Christmas temporarily forgot the children. The islanders are a friendly people, and I'm sure you would love them.

Just reading about your work helping people enjoy books makes us proud to be Americans, and we salute you. Writing about my experiences has helped me remember the adventures Helen and I have had together. Today my wife of 63 years reached her 82nd birthday, and we have never had a fight. I've had to defend myself a few times but who can argue for long with a beautiful woman?

I have mailed you a signed copy of my latest book under separate cover. It's a nonfiction adventure story of a CIA Contract Agent during 2½ years of the Vietnam War. During part of this period we lived on a Thai Firebase called Bearcat while I flew a Chinook for the 1st Cavalry Division. I also played Santa Clause for the Vietnamese orphans that Helen helped. "Confession of a CIA Interrogator" is not a children's book but maybe it should be required reading for those who are against the President and want to give up.

For God and Country,

DR. BEN R. GAMES PhD.

Ben R. Games, PhD

Honorable Vern Buchanan
House of Representatives 13 Dist.
Washington D.C. 20515   4 May 2007

Ref: Your letter dtd 1 May 2007 Ben R. Games, PhD. Purple Heart.

Dear Vern,

Do not worry about the Veteran Administration's letter to your office dated 2 April 2007 as it is a little misleading. The VA Decision Letter dated dtd 3 October 2006 recognized my combat injuries received when I was shot down during a firefight on the 8th Nov 1969. They also reviewed the medical records of when I was shot causing a lung to collapsed in Vietnam. The VA increased my disability to 100% and rated me as a Combat Veteran under the provisions of 38 CFR 3.304 (d).

The US Army Physical Disability Agency knew of my combat injuries and has been paying CRSC pay since 1 January 2004. The VA has a copy of the Army ruling that my combat related disability is now 60%. Mr. Barry M. Barker, Director of the VA Regional Office in ST Petersburg, FL may never have realized that the information he gave you was old and had been corrected.

His office referred me to the Department of the Army, US Army Resources Command, Lt/Colonel Sylvia A. Bennett, Military Awards Branch, 200 Stovall Street, Alexandria, VA 22332 for award of the Purple Heart. I have attached a copy of my letter to the Awards Branch. According to the Awards Branch many of the men who were wounded and died on the missions I was involved in were not historically a casualty of the Vietnam War.

                For God and Country,

                                            DR. BEN R. GAMES PhD.

A Cry for Help

Honorable Vern Buchanan
Attn: Staff Assistant Ms Joan Hansen
235 N. Orange Ave Suite#201
Sarasota, FL 34236   5 May 2007

Ref: Phone conversation 17 May 2007, Joan & Ben.

Dear Joan,

I received a letter from Vern with an attachment prepared and signed by the VA Director Mr. Barry M. Barker of the Veterans Regional Office in St Petersburg, Fl concerning your work on my behalf. I answered the Honorable Vern Buchanan letter with copies of the VA documents that they provide me. Please inform Vern that I have no problem with the VA as they have recognized my combat service and have rated my disabilities at 100%.

Please let him know that I was a soldier and will always be a soldier. I support all Veterans regardless of their being Democrats or Republicans. I also agree with President Abraham Lincoln writings, quote; "Congressmen who willfully take action during wartime to damage morale, and undermine the military are saboteurs. They should be arrested, exiled, or hanged."

The letter Mr. Barker wrote Vern had one major flaw; the information in the letter was copies of paragraphs taken from letters that the VA had written over the past two years. All the concerns had been resolved and corrected by the Veterans Administration. The VA even stated in one letter that their computers were not compromised but the errors had been done by one of their employees. I assume they fired the person responsible as I didn't hear anything about a hanging.

I hate it when someone tries to miss lead a Congressman or lies to a Senator. Maybe Vern can help give the US Army Awards Branch the authority to accept the VA & Army Physical Disability Agency (CRSC) findings as proof for issuing a Purple Heart without further requirements; so President John F. Kennedy's Executive Order, 25 April 1962, extending eligibility to any military or civilian national of the United States can be honored.

Copy: VFW

                    For God & Country,

                                                    DR. BEN R. GAN... ...D.

Ben R. Games, PhD

Department of the Army
Military Awards Branch, 200 Stovall St.
Alexander, VA 22332-0400 26 August 2007

Ref: Recommendation for the Purple Heart, US Army David L. Walker, Sgt (T) SSN# 390-42-2419, 1020 10th Ave W, suite#110, Palmetto, FL 34221.

Dear Lt/Col Sylvia Bennett,

I am aware that it is unusual for a retired field grade officer to recommend a soldier for an award years after the action occurred. Specialist Walker was injured in a firefight when the Slick UH-1D helicopter was shot down while inserting him and his Squad into a hot LZ in Tay Ninh Province, Vietnam. He sustained a back injury with various cuts and bruises. A field medic treated the wounds while he engaged the enemy and held them at bay.

Unfortunately he is another of the soldiers who are not on the Historical Casualty List of the Vietnam War. Also the Veterans Administration contends that the soldiers must have received a wound which necessitates treatment by a medical officer. Sergeant Walker's combat injuries occurred because the North Vietnamese would not stop trying to kill everyone while a medic treated his injuries so no paper record for the VA.

From personal experience I can testify that when someone is shooting at you the last thing on your mind is getting a piece of paper signed by the enemy saying he's trying to kill you or getting a medic to fill out a DA medical report. President John F. Kennedy on April 25th 1962 and President Ronald Reagan on February 23rd 1984 each issued an executive order for issuing the Purple Heart to civilians and soldiers during the Vietnam War.

I have flown an helicopter into LZ Burt, Tay Ninh Province many times, and once received enemy fire when I had soldiers aboard. When the firefight ended I had a collapsed lung from a bullet but was able to fly again two days later. Using a helicopter from "E" Battery, 82nd Artillery, 1st Cavalry Division I hit the enemy's latrines just at daybreak. My after action report read, "Caught the enemy with their pants down. When I left they were in a lot of shit." The mission was classified and the DA Form 759 was sanitized.

Ben R. Games, PhD, US Army Major (Ret)

Dr. Ben R. Games, PhD
814 Church St # 102
Ellenton, FL 34222

A Cry for Help

From: Mr. Joseph B. Kelly
808 Alison Drive
Jonesborough, TN 37659

Phone: 423-753-2009

1 September 2007

Ref: Confession of a CIA Interrogator

To: Fideli Publishing Inc.
9205 W. Old St. Rd. 67
Paragon, IN 46166

1 Sept 2007

Dear Sirs,

Dr. Games has informed me that your company has been retained to edit the book "Confession of a CIA Interrogator" author Ben R. Games, PhD, and to produce a 2nd printing as a collector's Hard Cover Book. Sarah my deceased wife and I edited the first printing to assure that the FACTS were true.

I understand that you will be attempting to sell the story to movie producers and to other Publishers. I was the CIA Contract Agent (Gilbert H. Moriggia) in the story, and was also present when the author interviewed Lt/Col Geoffrey T. Barker. I also allowed Ben access to my CIA documents, tapes, films, pictures, and passports to help verify parts of the story. I am available to act as Technical Advisor for any company purchasing this nonfiction story to produce a documentary.

The author and I first met on Okinawa in 1950, and our paths crossed many times thereafter as we worked around the world. We are friends but most people don't realize that he has also been known as Paper Doll, Longhorn 15, TCNA 6, and Gentle Ben or that he was a Nuclear Weapons Officer besides supporting my operations.

Sincerely,

Copy

USAF Retired, FE Division, CIA RVN

Ben R. Games, PhD

DEPARTMENT OF THE AIR FORCE
AIR UNIVERSITY (AETC)

10 September 2007

Ben R. Games, Ph.D.
814 Church St., Ste. #102
Ellenton FL 34222

Office of History (AU/HO)
60 Schumacher Ave., Ste. 3
Maxwell AFB AL 36112-6337

Dear Dr. Games,

Please forgive the delay in responding; we have had some personnel losses that make it difficult to process materials as quickly as we would like.

I am in receipt of your manuscript memoir entitled "A Terrorist's Mirror," which you were kind enough to provide to Air University. This is a well-written and valuable contribution, and all the more so because of its genuine 'first hand' perspective.

Given its subject matter, I have taken the liberty of forwarding your text to Air University's Fairchild Research Information Center (formerly AU Library) for possible accession. That would ensure your contribution is properly credited, indexed and cataloged for use by future researchers.

I would be remiss if I did not also suggest another possible repository for your memoir. If you are not familiar with their major effort to collect first-hand accounts of U.S. servicemens' experiences during the Vietnam War, then you may wish to contact:

    Vietnam Center & Archive
    Texas Tech University
    P. O. Box 41045
    Lubbock TX 79409-1045
    (806) 742-3742

Again, please let me express my appreciation for your thoughtful efforts to record 'a military moment in time' …and to thank you for your service to our Nation.

With best wishes,

George W. Cully
Director

A Cry for Help

Board for Correction of Military Records
Director, Catherine C. Mitrano
1901 South Bell Street 2nd Floor
Arlington, VA 22202-4508   1 October 2007

Ref: Docket Date: 11 September 2007 #AR20070005607, Games, Ben R.,
         PhD, Major (USAF & USA), CW4 (USA), TCNA-6.

Dear Board Members;

Thank you for considering and reviewing my request for the Purple Heart award. I request the award because I truly believed that a Presidential Executive Order could not be changed or restricted by military regulations. I was wrong, and you have done me no harm in refusing this request.

I am sure that you have not been on the receiving end of a 51 Cal machinegun or fell 800 feet in flames or you would be wondering why I would volunteer to go back in combat on the 9 November 1969. That's exactly what my wife Helen asked me. If you had read the complete Medical Examination dated 15 May 1970 you would have seen where my combat injuries were recorded. Nurses and doctors always ask how much pain, and I ask when. Right now is always their answer. If I don't move there is no pain so I haven't lied. On the 8 Nov 69 when my Chinook was shot down I was 45 yrs, 6 months, 3 days old, and hate it when someone is shooting at me.

In 1967 I was a major in the USAF and we lived in the Ashia Hotel, Bangkok, Thailand and traveled in South Vietnam, Cambodia, and Laos before returning to Detroit where I flew General Ward during the riots. 1968 I was assigned to Ft Rucker to check out in Army helicopters. 1969 to February 1970 we lived on a Thai Firebase called Bear Cat. The request to separate in Vietnam was only a cover story as I still had internal bleeding from injuries received during the firefight at LZ Vivian. The assignment to the 34th General Support Group was also to give me time to recover from my injures so I could continue my assignment. It didn't. help. Helen was flown home and three days later I was medivaced by air.

My service and award of the Bronze Star by "E" Bt, 82nd Art, 1st Cav. was not mentioned in your letter. Maybe that was one of the medals you couldn't understand. I have enclosed a copy of two manuscripts that might help.

Ben R. Games, PhD

During research for the book "Confession of a CIA Interrogator" I located a Sp-4 David L. Walker and a Joseph B. Kelly who had been wounded but did not receive a Purple Heart. I understand that I am not a historical causality but I do not believe its fair not to give the award to soldiers who were wounded or killed fighting with me. Both of the men's names I've written here continued fighting after they were wounded and are not historical causalities either but they were men who did not give up.

The Board did determine that there were administration errors in my records and indicated that they will be corrected. If it was about our being medivaced on the Hospital ship USS Hope at the end of WWII or service with the Air National Guard, or when I was with the USAF and we lived on Chambley Air Base, France it is not necessary as I know about these.

I was aware that the DD214 issued for the period when I was shot down and injured was for seven months of Vietnam's one year duty tour because I needed medical attention. My retirement from active duty on 1 January 1978 was made so the VA could get me ready for an assignment where I had to be listed as a civilian so I could fight the Drug Cartels from Columbia without involving the military. Support was provided by island police and a British Frigate. I was actually retired from the US Army on 11 February 1987.

Anything you can due to recognize the two men I have named above would honor the US Army. I am truly sorry that the families of soldiers in the body bags I dropped off at the Saigon Mortuary Pad will never know that they were true heroes. I never realized that they were not historically casualties.

This letter is not a request for you to reopen my file, but only my apology for causing the Board to waste their time.

Inc.   For God and Country;
"The Bangkok Drop"
"A Terrorist Mirror"

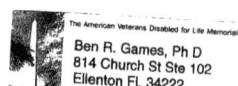

The American Veterans Disabled for Life Memorial
Ben R. Games, Ph D
814 Church St Ste 102
Ellenton FL 34222

A Cry for Help

Joseph B. Kelly
808 Alison Drive
Jonesborough, TN 37649   8 October 2007

Ref: Purple heart.

Dear Joe,

Here are copies of the letters that were used trying to get the Military Awards Branch to issue you a Purple Heart.

I will not send or keep any further correspondence on this matter as I know it must be causing tension with your family. On my latest round of arguments I was pleased when they accepted your medical records of the wounds and injuries. The award was turned down because military regulations require that you must have applied within in three (3) years of the incident. They also produced a letter that you had written claming you were a CIA Contract Officer and not a civilian employee.

I answered the Board's Decision letter on the 1st October 2007. I will not send you copies or my strategy so if it doesn't work it's my fault and if it does you will only receive what you rightly deserve.

                 For God and Country,

                                            DR. BEN R. GAMES PhD.

Ben R. Games, PhD

Department of the Army
Board for Correction of Military Records
1901 South Bell Street 2nd Floor
Arlington, VA 22202-4508   18 January 2008

Ref: AR20050007776 and AR20070005607, Games, Ben R., Major. Request for Reconsideration Award of the Purple Heart.

Dear Sirs;

I hereby request reconsideration, and my letter dtd 1 October 2007 be made part of this request. Also that my manuscripts "The Bangkok Drop & A Terrorist Mirror" with documentation to be part of the file.

My letter dated 1 October 2007 stated that it was not a request to reopen my file. This was true as I do not serve our country for awards or medals. However, when I showed the letter of Denial from the Army Board for Correction of Military Records to Mr. Kenneth A. Thie, Director, VFW Veterans Service Officer it was brought to my attention that I do not have the right to deprive recognition for those soldiers who were wounded or died while we were in firefights with the enemy.

When someone is shooting at me it makes me mad, and my only interest is to brake away from their fire and attack. I do not believe in making a body count of the enemy dead as they are of no danger to me after the firefight is over. I have never left a wounded or dead American soldier on the Battle Field. In Vietnam I never knew the US Army had an official "Casualty List" or that a solider had be on the list to be recognized.

I will submit a rebuttal of the Boards decision with newspaper clippings, documents, medical records, and photographs.

Inc: VFW BIO by
     Vicky Lopez

                For God and Country;

                                       DR. BEN R. GAMES PhD.

A Cry for Help

US Human Resource Command
Lt/Col Sylvia A. Bennett, Chief
Military Awards Branch, 200 Stovall Street
Alexandria, VA 22332-0400   10 February 2008

Ref: Your letter 6 March 2007, Ben R. Games, PhD, Major, CW4 (Ret)

Dear Lt/Col Bennett;

A DD Form 149 for correction of military records was submitted. The ABCMR Board denied the request for the following reasons. First, they thought that I really knew that there was a three year time limit on corrections. Second, that my name was not on the official "Vietnam Casualty List." Third, they informed me that it could not be determined from the medical records if it was enemy or friendly fire.

They did add three medals from Vietnam that were not listed on my retirement DD214. They were correct in one thing though. We had to fight on the ground as well as in the air, and weren't rescued until after all the enemy were killed. Someone took a picture of two Viet Cong who were dressed in white shirts and dark pants who were scouting for the North Vietnamese Army. I was not interested in dead enemy soldiers as they were no longer a threat to my crew or passengers.

The Veterans Administration spent a lot of years researching my medical records before suggesting the Department of Defense may want to authorize the Purple Heart. Army medical records indicate it was ten hours after I was shot before receiving surgical procedures to inflate my lung. My other combat injures were corrected in military and VA hospitals over a period of years. The Board also referred to my Class II Army physical at Fort Rucker where I wrote, "I am in good health" but didn't put down the statement written on Line 34 referring to my combat injuries. In fact they never wrote anything about receiving a Bronze Star from "E" Bt, 82nd Artillery or the other times I was injured from enemy fire.

I have enclosed a copy of the "Army Correction of Records Rebuttal" submitted to the ABCMR Board for your consideration.

                    Sincerely,

                                        DR. BEN R. GAMES

Ben R. Games, PhD

Army Review Board Agency
Mr. Walter Avery, Chief
Case Management Division
1901 South Bell Street
Arlington, VA 22202-4508   15 February 2008

Ref: Case Number AR20080002197, Games, Ben R.; PhD, Maj, CW4.

Dear Mr. Avery;

Thank you for the letter assigning a Case Number to my request. I have been sending different Thesis written for the USAF University, US Army War College, and Carlisle Barracks along with 126 pages of medical records in support of the request for correction of ABCMR's report.

The Veterans Administration spent years researching my medical records before they realized mine wasn't a normal soldier's life. The VA military medical records cover a period of 44 years 4 month, 28 days of military service and are over a 1000 pages.

Mr. Kenneth A. Thie, Director VFW Service Office, PO Box 1437 (Rm 217A) has copies of some of the actual DD Form 759 and USAF Form 5's. The military orders of some of my assignments during WWII are at the Army War College and others are at the USAF Air University. Some are classified. I am aware that some of the records have been sanitized or rebuilt to support new assignments. The requested for the Purple Heart was made when I learned that the men who were killed or wounded serving with me including myself were not on the official Vietnam Casualty List.

I have already sent the following Theses: The Bangkok Drop, A Terrorist Mirror, VFW Biography of Games by Vicki Lopez, Army Correction of Records; Rebuttal, and referred to research for books "Confession of a CIA Interrogator" (2007) "Jihad Vietnam" (2008). If any of these have been lost please notify me. I will replace them.

Written but not reread.

DR. BEN R. GAMES PhD.

A Cry for Help

Department of the Army
Board for Correction of Military Records
1901 South Bell Street 2nd Flour
Arlington, VA 22202-4508 ---- February 2008

Ref: AR20070005607, Games Ben R., Major, Request for Reconsideration of award of the Purple Heart dtd 20 September 2007.

Dear Sirs;
REBUTTAL OF BOARDS DECISION

Consideration of evidence: Title 10, section 1552 (b) requires that corrections must be filed within 3 yrs after discovery of an error. The Board alleges that it appears the applicant did not file in the authorized time frame.

Rebuttal of Evidence listed 1 through 24.

> The undersigned admits that he did not consider medical records important until he was doing research as the author for the book titled "Confession of a CIA Interrogator" © 2007. In 2006 the author discovered that medical records of Joseph B. Kelly, S/Sgt USAF (ret), Vietnam Police Advisor, were classified secret, Dave L Walker, Sgt SP5 US Army was treated by field medics during combat.
>
> The undersigned was aware that his personal military and medical records were sanitized or classified secret to prevent his missions from becoming known by the enemy. The Bronze Star was awarded without the "V" device so that no record of the missions need be recorded.
>
> He also states that he did not know that President Kennedy's Executive Order for the award of the Purple Heart included civilian and military personnel injured or killed fighting the enemy until 17 November 2005. ABCMR determination that the statue of limitations for timely filing should be wavered in the interest of justice is correct.
>
> The request for reconsideration is made this 20th day of January 2008 within one year from the Boards records of Proceedings dated 11th day

of September 2007. Upon favorable consideration the undersigned agrees to resubmit a request for award of the Purple Heart to the Army Award Branch for those soldiers who's records were located during research for the book "Jihad Vietnam by Ben R. Games, PhD 2008". Their names are not on the Official Vietnam Casualty List.

Records during the period from 15 June 1955 to 30 September 1962 are in error. Applicant served on active duty as a fighter pilot in the USAF Air Defense Command, Indiana Air National, and as a USAF Major, Chambley Air Field, France. They lived in USAF base housing.

The undersigned served as a commissioned officer with the USAF from November 1962 to June 1967 as a Nuclear Safety Officer, Disaster Control Officer, Aircraft Accident Investigation Officer, Recruiting Officer, and as an USAF advisor to the Thai Marine Police in Bangkok, Thailand.

Your records during the period 11 June 1969 to February 1970 is in error. The General Order Number 718 should also include "VOCO assignment to "E" Battery 82nd Artillery, 1st Cavalry Division. A Bronze Star was awarded by "E" Battery 82nd Artillery to the undersigned. The missions were highly classified. Ref: The Terrorist Mirror, and the book "Confession of a CIA Interrogator by Ben R. Games, PhD."

The undersigned was shot down 4 times during firefights with the enemy in Vietnam. Helen lived on the Thai firebase in a 26 ft trailer behind the American PX. After the firefight on the 8th November 1969 She had him flown to the USAF Hospital at Phuoc Vinh Air Base, and his lung was inflated. All ruptures and other damage was repaired by USAF hospitals or the VA between assignments. All combat medical records in Vietnam were sanitized, classified secret, or destroyed.

On 26 November 1969 request to be separated in Bien Hoa was part of a plan to provide time for the undersigned to recover from combat injuries without alerting the enemy that their attack was successful. Helen the undersigned's wife never lived in Bien Hoa. They lived in a trailer on the Thai Firebase called Bear Cat. His injures were so serious that he needed time to recover so he could continue with his combat assignments.

On the 4th December 1969 the assignment to the 34th General Support Group was not made. The Battalion Flight Surgeon approved the transfer to help give time for his injuries to heal so he could continue his mission assignment. The wounds proved too serious, and they were flown to the Fort Rucker, Hospital on the 5th February 1970.

Records indicating duty at Fort Rucker on 5 February 1970 are in error. The undersigned was under the care of US Army medical doctors and failed his Class II physical. He performed no military duties.

In a report of a medical examination dated 15 May 1970 where the applicant stated that there had been no change in his mental or physical health condition is correct. The same medical report clearly stated in his handwriting that he was still suffering pain from combat injuries received when his Chinook was shot down at LZ Vivian, Vietnam.

The undersigned has requested the Veterans Administration to make copies of his military medical records for your consideration. Many of the records have been sanitized, destroyed, or lost but the VFW has been informed that the file is in two volumes each over four 4" thick covering WWII, Korean War, Berlin Crises, and Vietnam. These files will be mailed to you for your review. The VA says that it will take four months or longer to prepare and the veteran must pay for the copies.

Newspaper clippings, documents, and photographs will also be mailed separately.

Inc; VFW BIO by
    Vicky Lopez

Copy of letter to:
Representative Vern Buchanan
Senator Mel Martinez
Senator Bill Nelson

Military Awards Branch

        For God and Country;   DR. BEN R. GAMES PhD.

Ben R. Games, PhD

DEPARTMENT OF THE ARMY
U.S. ARMY HUMAN RESOURCES COMMAND
200 STOVALL STREET
ALEXANDRIA VA 22332-0400

February 28, 2008

VFW

We'd do anything for this country!

Military Awards Branch

Dr. Ben R. Games
814 Church Street #102
Ellenton, Florida 34222-2318

Dear Dr. Games:

    This is in response to your letter of August 26, 2007, concerning your desire to recommend Mr. David L. Walker for a Purple Heart for injuries he received in the Republic of Vietnam.

    The National Personnel Records Center maintains the Official Personnel Files of Army veterans and is the agency responsible for the replacement of medals for veterans and retirees. The National Personnel Records Center will review Mr. Walker's file and authorize issuance of the Purple Heart if he is entitled. If the center is unable to determine his eligibility for any awards, they will forward pertinent documentation to this office for review and final determination. We have enclosed Standard Form 180 (Request Pertaining to Military Records) so that Mr. Walker may request the information himself. Alternately, he may use the form to allow you to request record information on his behalf. He may write to their office at:

National Personnel Records Center
9700 Page Avenue
St. Louis, MO 63132-5100

    When writing to the National Personnel Records Center, Mr. Walker should provide them a copy of his DD Form 214 (Report of Separation) because in July 1973, the center suffered a catastrophic fire that destroyed many of our veterans' military records.

    Thank you for your interest in the Army's Awards Program.

Sincerely,

Sylvia A. Bennett LTC, AG
Lieutenant Colonel, U.S. Army
Chief, Military Awards Branch

Enclosures

A Cry for Help

Lt/Col Sylvia A. Bennett, USA
Chief, Military Awards Branch
200 Stovall Street
Alexandria, VA 22332-0471   6 March 2008

Ref: Your letter 28 February 2008.

Dear Sylvia,

My reader indicated that it appeared someone besides yourself signed the referred to letter. If it truly represents your thinking then you may have been mislead by someone on your staff.

The military records were sanitized at the time for protection of the missions. I have no desire to disclose these assignments, and do not believe that they should be made public. Somehow I let your office convince me to submit a request for correction of military records. It must have been old age as normally I can recognize when someone is just passing the buck.

I know about the Bronze Star Medal for meritorious service. This was awarded by "E" Bt, 82nd Artillery, 1st Cav Div so no record of my work would need to be recorded. I would never ask that the Bronze Star be down graded. In fun I've written about some of my non-classified missions stating that it could have been issued for these. Please read the theses written for the USAF Air University named; A Terrorist Mirror and the Bangkok Drop.

Your second paragraph; Quote, "We place trust in our field commanders to make these decisions because they have firsthand knowledge of the deeds performed by Soldiers of his unit." I am sure you do, and it makes sense to me. The statement also makes good reading but my hard missions never came through any Company or Battalion Commander. Then ask yourself how could a soldier remain in the service for over 40 years with these combat injuries plus having the State Department authorized his family to live in every war zone he worked in. Once during the Korean War the assignment was to an Army Engineer Battalion who's commander could only find me at the Officer's Club, and never discovered that his battalion was only a cover for my missions. Another time I saved a USAF Wing Commander's career by getting the French Government to issue a prostitute ID card for his wife so she could attend a French government functions. My secret orders from the

Ben R. Games, PhD

USAF Chief of Staff were to make sure that he didn't violate President Kennedy's orders that family members could not attend. The French do not consider a prostitute a member of the family. The Chief of Staff thought it was funny the way I had solved the problem. The Wing Commander's wife never forgave me.

Helen attended combat training with Army nurses at Fort Rucker before we left for our 2nd trip to Vietnam. Our son Jon and one of his classmates at Culver Military Academe attended combat training at Ft Rucker. Our son was 16 yrs old when he joined us in Vietnam during Christmas vacation and flew combat missions as a pilot in a UH-1 helicopter.

My concern is still for the men who fought with me and were wounded but not counted as historical casualties. I can provide the medical records showing that Joseph B. Kelly was injured in a mortar attack, and SP4 David Walker was treated by a field medic and received the Bronze Star for Valor. Maybe one of your staff can ask the IG to read them President Kennedy's Executive Order of 1962. I am sending a copy of this letter to our Commander in Chief in the hope that he will strengthen all Presidential Executive Orders.

For God and Country,

Copy to: President G. Bush.

DR. BEN R. GAMES PhD.

A Cry for Help

President George Bush
White House
1600 Pennsylvania Ave
Washington DC, 20500

8 March 2008

Ref: Presidential Executive Order.

Honorable President Bush,

Helen and I want you to know that you have our full support. We don't think that anyone could served America better. After living in many countries including some war zones we understand what you must have gone through during the 9/11 attack upon our country.

I have read President Kennedy's Executive Order (1962) that referred to the award of the Purple Heart. Our concerns are not just for the wounded soldiers but for all citizens who believe that a Presidential Executive Order should not be changed by individuals for their own political agenda. Senator Kerry understood Navy regulations and used them to avoid fighting America's enemies. While I do not agree with what he did; Navy Regulation were not violated. If the Navy had not changed the intent of President Kennedy's Executive Order he may not have been successful.

I have received letters form Lt/Col Sylvia A. Bennett, Chief, Army Military Awards Branch. She has been writing about Army restrictions against awarding the Purple Heart for a few men who served with me in Vietnam. After receiving letters with answers that seemed counter to the intent of a Presidential Executive Order I started using my own combat injuries to learn what was needed because they had been verified by the Veterans Administration.

There is no need to issue me a Purple Heart, but if these men who continued fighting for our country after being wounded were recognized it would do the Army Proud. Anything you can do to strengthen a Presidential Executive Order will help all veterans.

For God and Country,

PhD Ben R Games
Suite 102
814 Church St
Ellenton FL 34222-2318

Ben R. Games, PhD

Department of the Army
Board for Correction of Military Records
Director, Catherine C. Mitrano
1901 South Bell Street 2nd Floor
Arlington, VA 22202-4508

5 June 2008

Ref: AR20080002197, Games.

Dear Ms Mitrano,

I received your letter dated 14 May 2008, and the Vietnam Gallantry Cross with Palm Citation Badge, also the Republic of Vietnam Civil Actions Honor Medal, plus the First Class Unit Citation Badge.

Thanks for your suggestion.

Today is our 65th wedding anniversary and we would like to give you a copy of my latest book called "Jihad Vietnam".

For God and Country,

DR. BEN R. GAMES PhD.

A Cry for Help

Mr. Art Overman
1116 Las Posas
San Clemente, CA 92673

22 November 2008

Dear Art,

Sorry for the delay in answering your question about my estimate on our economy. In my opinion this crises was part of a terrorist attack upon our system of government. In many of my writings I refer to the Communist introducing the anti-Christ sign as the Pease Sign. It was a plan of the North Vietnamese minister of information Mr. Cat Lee around 1962 and later introduced into the United States by Senator John Kerry. Today the dollar sign seems to be taking its place.

In the late 1950s I attended Geo-Economics classes at Notre Dame University in South Bend, Indiana. as part of our military's graduate studies. I am still amazed at the accuracy of the GDP projections fifty years later. I've found that the only thing that has changed is today it is called, "Global Economy."

I'm sorry but I have no quick fix as there are many variables that must be considered. In 2004 I started changing our investments to meet my belief of a future financial meltdown. Helen my wife has a MBA in business and doesn't always agree with me but so far I've guessed right.

Professor Timothy Taylor of Macalester College is the Managing Editor of Journal of Economic Perspectives and has recorded lectures on CD's for "The Teaching Company, 4151 Lafayette Center Drive, Suite 100, Chantilly, Virginia 20151-1232. Phone 1-800-TEACH-12. His lectures on America and the New Global Economy should help you plan for the future and your guess of how long it will last. I'm planning for two to three years before the bottom is reached and then almost a level GDP for another five years.

For God and Country,

DR. BEN R. GAMES PhD

Ben R. Games, PhD

Commander-in-Chief President Bush
White House, 1600 Pennsylvania Ave
Washington D.C. 20500

26 December 2008

Ref: Donation for your Presidential Library.

Dear Sir,

I am a military retired life member of the Distinguished Flying Cross Society. As you know the DFC is the same for all branches of the military services and for all ranks. Your father can tell you about when he earned his DFC during WWII. I earned mine during the Vietnam War.

I would like to donate a DFC Unit FLAG, the book Jihad Vietnam, and a Plaque telling what the DFC medal is and how it came to be. In your museum It would fit in with the story of your service as a jet fighter pilot in the Texas Air National Guard. The gifts value is $250 dollars but I could ask for a DFCS list of the individuals from Texas who also hold the award.

If you can except the gift please provide me with your Curator's name and the location where to send the items.

For God and Country,

[signature: Ben R. Games]

Ben R. Games, Ph.D
814 Church St Suite #102
Ellenton, FL 34222-2318

A Cry for Help

Honorable Vern Buchanan
1516 Longworth House Office Building
Washington D.C.   20515   17 February 2009

Dear Vern,

Thanks for your personal letter dtd 2 February 2009. My answer to your question is that the two US Border Guards should have been paid a bonus, given a medal, and promoted. In 1980 before the military had police powers I was sent to the Caribbean to stop drugs from being transported on TCNA (Nation Airline) planes.

Soon after I arrived a convicted drug smuggler and murder was captured by the police, and I was asked to transport him to the court on another island. I had the man placed in leg irons with hands fastened behind his back. Then I used duck tape to hold the trigger back on my young native policemen's shotgun. The prisoner was seated in the back facing forward and strapped in with duck tape facing the policeman. Next the duck tape was used to hold the shotgun's barrel into his mouth; yes it was loaded. The flight was only going to take an hour but from the look on the prisoner and guard's face they must both have thought it was going to be forever. Just before take off I pulled back the hammer of the policeman's weapon and told him that if he let go he would have to clean the plane.

There was really no danger to the aircraft as we never flew higher than 2000 feet, and there were no passengers. I was not in court for the hearing but the Judge told the Commissioner of Police that the prisoner had not killed any of their people and only five Americans in the United States. The Americans had lost the prisoner once, and he was really their problem. The Judge then told the court that Americans did not like terrorists or drug smugglers, and the Commissioner should remember this the next time he needed prisoners moved. The Judge fined the prisoner one hundred thousand dollars, and three days later the drug cartel raided the prison to release him.

I have always liked duck tape and in Vietnam it was used to patch the bullet holes in my Chinook. Since then I've found many other uses for the sticky stuff.

                        For God and Country,   *signature*

                                                    Ben R. Games, Ph.D
                                                    814 Church St Suite #102
                                                    Ellenton, FL 34222-2318

Ben R. Games, PhD

Honorable Vern Buchanan
US Representative FL #13
Washington D.C. 20515

10 August 2009

Ref: Award of the Purple Heart.

Dear Vern,

A friend of mine Mr. Joseph B. Kelly is attempting to have his combat injuries in Vietnam recognized and to receive the Purple Heart. I also understand his Congressional Representative Phil Roe (TN #1) is trying to help him. I knew you struck out when your office tried to help me, but I'm hoping that his representative will be successful with your help.

Can you ask your aid who worked trying to help me explain the mistakes we made so they may avoid these pitfalls. If they are successful then may be the same procedure can be followed to help Mr. David Walker (AR Sgt) Manatee County FL (13) and other veterans of our District.

Now that Mr. John I. Kiener, Editor, Lifestyles, Herald & Tribune is writing a serial of the Vietnam War and about fighting in the shadows maybe people will become interested. (Copy Attached) To Be Continued

For God and Country,

DR. BEN R. GAMES PhD.

A Cry for Help

Honorable Phil Roe
US Representative, Tn #1
Washington D.C. 2015   10 August 2009

Ref; Purple Heart Awards for combat injuries received by Joseph B. Kelly.

Dear Sir,

I will support anything you can due to help Mr. Joseph B. Kelly in obtaining the award of the Purple Heart. I have flown with Joe and can attest to his being wounded twice in direct combat with North Vietnamese Army troops. I have also personally seen the medical records for the treatment of his wounds, and they were classified Secret.

When I learned that Lt/Col Sylvia A. Bennett US Army Chief, Military Awards Branch had two different lists for the award of the Purple Heart I resubmitted a recommendation of the award for Joseph B. Kelly because I had seen his secret combat metical records. I believe this was done by the State Department to prevent the American people from knowing that the North Vietnamese could attack an Embassy at anytime they wanted too.

This time I was informed by Lt/Col Bennett that Mr. Kelly was not on active duty at the time of the firefight even though he was receiving retired pay from the USAF and being paid by the US Army. His actions during the firefight helped prevent the overrun of the Embassy and saved the life of a US General Officer and the Vietnamese civilian employees of the State Department.

I am sending a copy of this letter to Representative Vern Buchanan, FL Dist. #13 asking him to support you in this matter.

For God and Country,

Dr. Ben R. Games, PhD
814 Church St # 102
Ellenton, FL 34222-2318

Ben R. Games, PhD

Edward Jones
2808 Manatee Ave West
Bradenton, FL 34205   14 September 2009

Ref: WWII, the poem "FUUJIN."

Dear Errol,

I find that your research is fantastically accurate. My stories are based upon notes written in my journal at the time it happened or maybe the next day. The trouble is that they are not mellowed by time and maybe colored by fear. On the plus side is Helen's and my age as we have been there. My writing is not to change history but only to tell what we did in it.

Before leaving on assignment to destroy a secret Japanese Laser Test Station facing the Sea of Japan I studied everything that I could find about the Japanese in the Manila Library. I discovered that they had over eight million Gods and if I counted Jesus Christ there were eight million and one that I had to consider. Their was only one or some will say two religions in Japan at that time. One was the Shinto's who had shrines were they could light Joss Sticks to "Hachiman (the Shinto God of War) and the others were Temples with a statue of Buddha in them. Buddha was a real person and not really counted as a religion by the Japanese. In fact they referred to the Shinto's worker as a Priest and called the Buddhist Temple leaders Monks with the buildings as Shrine-Temples. There were only two Japanese Gods that I was worried about during WWII. One was "Hachiman" and the other was "Fuujin".

One night I prayed to Jesus Christ asking Him to keep the other Gods off my back. I arrived in Japan the day before the surrender terms were signed, and it must have been with my Guardian Angel's help as I was able to outsmart Hatchiman as told in the story "Who Stole the Train?" and "The Divine Wind". Now the Japanese Okinawa God "Fuujin" was a good and bad God so I had to learn how to work with him.

A long time ago I wrote a poem that gives the answer to those who write asking questions about why it sometimes rains too much or too little.

For God and Country,   *[signature]*

Dr. Ben R. Games, PhD
814 Church St # 102
Ellenton, FL 34222-2318

FUUJIN

by Ben R. Games, PhD

The Great One created the Heaven and Earth. Then he built a Garden of Eden for his likeness. Then he rested. The next day he looked down upon his garden and saw that the trees, flowers, and meadows needed water for they were turning brown; so he created soft billowy clouds to rain upon them. Then he looked down again and saw that the ground had too much water and was turning into mud. God called the Archangel Michael and told him to think of some way to help His garden grow.

The Archangel formed a committee of Angels and told them that the Lord had said to help the garden grow. They decided that someone would have to move the clouds to where the rain was needed, help pollinate the flowers, and to help spread the seeds of all the plants. When the Lord heard of the plan he called out; "FUUJIN".

On warm days I gently rock the baby's cradle, dry the sweat from the man's brow, and move the clouds where they are needed to water the crops. I help move ships, and make high waves for the surfers. I help powered parachutes and trikes fly. I even help sail boats to win races. I make dust devils in dry fields and play with leaves in the fall. I am "FUUJIN"'

Upon God's order I moved the waters of the Red Sea. I can change the shape of Mountains, and create floods. I am on duty all the time. I seldom rest and I can change the winner of sail boat races just for fun. I can destroy crops, towns, or just one building. I can make a fisherman laugh or cry. I am "FUUJIN".

Some call me Typhoon, Hurricane, Tornado, Chinook, Thor, but no matter what I am called everyone knows me, loves me, hates me, and fears me. I am in charge of making the clouds move, and in helping God's children take care of the earth. I am the Okinawa God of Wind, I am, "FUUJIN".

A Cry for Help

Fuujin &
The 4th Fighter Squadron

The emblem of the 4th Fighter Squadron during the Korean War was Fuujin.

Fuujin, the Okinawa God of Wind, green, carrying a large yellow sack, wearing a red scarf draped about the neck and shoulders, all in front of a gray thunder cloud with yellow lighting flash and raindrops issuing towards Dexter base was approved as an emblem of the 4th Fighter Squadron by the USAF on 25 February 1949.

Ben R. Games, 1st Lt USAF was a fighter pilot flying the P-61s & F-82G in the 4th Fighter Squadron in 1949/50.

4TH FIGHTER SQUADRON LINEAGE

- Constituted the 4th Pursuit Squadron on 20 Nov 1940
- Activated on 15 Jan 1941
- Redesignated: 4th Fighter Squadron 15 May 1942
- Inactivated 7 Nov 1945
- Activated on 20 Feb 1947
- Redesignated: 4th Fighter Squadron (All Weather) on 10 Aug 1948
- 4th Fighter Squadron All Weather on 20 Jan 1950
- 4th Fighter-Interception Squadron on 25 Apr 1951.

DURING WW-II

- Combat Operations ETO & MTO

CAMPAIGNS

Air Offensive: Europe, Algeria-French, Morocco, Tunisia, Sicily, Naples Apennines; Rhineland, Central Europe, Po Valley, Air Combat EAME Theater.

AIRCRAFT

- P-40
- P-39
- Spitfire
- P-51.

STATIONS DURING 1949 & 1950

Naha, Okinawa & Misawa, Japan.

AIRCRAFT ASSIGNED DURING THIS PERIOD

P-61 and F-82G

OPERATIONS

Combat Air defense of the Ryukyus Islands during the Korean War.

Ben R. Games, PhD

DAVID P. ROE
1ST DISTRICT, TENNESSEE

EDUCATION AND LABOR
AGRICULTURE
VETERANS' AFFAIRS

COUNTIES:
CARTER
COCKE
GREENE
HAMBLEN
HANCOCK
HAWKINS
JEFFERSON
JOHNSON
SEVIER
SULLIVAN
UNICOI
WASHINGTON

Congress of the United States
House of Representatives
Washington, DC 20515–4201

October 6, 2009

The Honorable Hilda Solis
Secretary
United States Department of Labor
200 Constitution Avenue, Northwest
Room S-2018
Washington, DC 20210-0002

COPY

Dear Secretary Solis,

    Joseph B. Kelly, a constituent of the First Congressional District of Tennessee, was employed by the Central Intelligence Agency and stationed in Southeast Asia during the conflict in Viet Nam. During his employment there he suffered injuries resulting from attacks by enemy forces.

    In 2002 the Central Intelligence Agency agreed to compensate Mr. Kelly for hearing loss resulting from one of these attacks. To date he has not been compensated for other injuries he sustained, including a diagnosis of Post Traumatic Stress Disorder made during an examination at the James H. Quillen V.A. Medical Center. Because Mr. Kelly was a CIA employee and not in military service at the time of the attacks he has been denied service-connected compensation by the Department of Veterans Affairs for his injuries. In addition, Mr. Kelly believes he is eligible to be awarded Purple Hearts for these injuries as he was at the time performing peace keeping duties in Viet Nam.

    Any information your agency can provide Mr. Kelly as to how to proceed with claims for compensation will be greatly appreciated. I am enclosing all relevant documents Mr. Kelly has provided related to his injuries. Also, proof of his service in Viet Nam and the injuries sustained there will be beneficial to his claim for the Purple Heart with the Department of Defense and I would ask that you provide any suggestion on how to obtain this information.

    I appreciate your service and look forward to your reply.

Sincerely,

David P. Roe
Member of Congress TN-01

WASHINGTON
419 CANNON HOUSE OFFICE BUILDING
WASHINGTON, DC 20515
PHONE: 202-225-6356
FAX: 202-225-5714

KINGSPORT HIGHER EDUCATION CENTER
205 REVERE STREET
KINGSPORT, TN 37660

MAILING ADDRESS:
POST OFFICE BOX 1728
PHONE: 423-247-8161
FAX: 423-247-0119

ON THE CAMPUS OF WALTERS STATE
1609 COLLEGE PARK DRIVE, SUITE 4
MORRISTOWN, TN 37813
PHONE: 423-254-1400
FAX: 423-254-1403

PRINTED ON RECYCLED PAPER
www.roe.house.gov

A Cry for Help

President Barack Obama
1600 Pennsylvania Ave
Washington D.C. 20050

24 November 2009

Honorable President Obama,

Would you please consider providing a letter authorizing the wearing of the Vietnamese Wound Medal. Only American award were placed on the DD214 at the time of discharge. All the soldiers including myself are members of the VFW and receive VA compensation. No funds are involved only recognition

My name is Ben R. Games, PhD, Major, CW-4, 1st Cavalry Division, III Corps, Senior Army Aviator, Company "B", 228th Av Bn & "E" Bt 82nd Artillery. I suffered combat injuries once during WWII and twice during the Vietnam War. Awarded the Distinguished Flying Cross for heroism.

I would like to recommend T/Sgt Joseph B. Kelly, Army Providence Officer for the US Army, and Sgt David L. Walker of firebase Burt who were wounded but wouldn't stop fighting to receive authorization to wear the Vietnamese Wound Medal.

On Christmas day 1969 my Chinook lifted a rope with a 100 dead North Vietnamese soldiers at LZ Burt to a trench so they could be counted before burial. I also flew many Snatch and Grab missions in Vietnam for Joseph B. Kelly while he was working as a Province Officer for the US Army.

David L. Walker, BS, Sgt, US Army, LZ Burt, Vietnam, 3rd Battalion, 22nd Infantry Operation Diamondhead. Was wounded 1 January 1968, and received the Bronze Star for Valor. The Firebase was overrun but Sgt Walker wouldn't stop fighting or surrender. As punishment his Company Commander would not award the Purple Heart and made him perform the body count. He is a personal friend and has assisted me by providing some pictures for my nonfiction book, "Confession of a CIA Interrogator".

       David L. Walker
       North River Builders Inc
       1020 10 Ave W. Suite 110
       Palmetto, FL 34221

Ben R. Games, PhD

Joseph B. Kelly, T/Sgt, USAF retired and worked for the US Army as a Vietnam Police Advisor (GS 11) in Kien Hoa Province. He was wounded while defending the American Embassy on the night of 7th June and 8th June 1970. He organized the defense of the Embassy, and refused treatment for his wounds until after the fighting stopped. The attack on the American Embassy was classified Secret as was the medical records of Mr. Kelly. The medical report states that Joseph B. Kelly was a GS-11 employee of the US labor department at the time he was wounded.

I have known Mr. Kelly from when he took care of my survival gear at Naha, Okinawa during 1949. I was flying a P-61A Black Widow with the 4th Night Fighter Squadron from Naha on missions over China at the time.

Mr. Joseph B. Kelly
808 Alison Drive
Jonesborough, TN 37659

According to Lt/Col Sylvia A. Bennett, US Army Chief, Military Awards Branch none of the individuals including myself received the Purple Heart as we were not on the approved list. Someone may have to remind her that the Vietnamese Wound Medal is not under her jurisdiction.

With your approval I will volunteer to purchase the medals and request the VFW to present them. There will be no funding required.

For God and Country,

Ben R. Games

Ben R. Games, Ph.D
814 Church St Suite #102
Ellenton, FL 34222-2318

A Cry for Help

Honorable Vern Buchanan
US Representative FL-13
Washington, D.C. 20515   14 December 2009

Dear Vern,

Somehow I've misplaced your reply to my request for support of Honorable David P. Roe ® TN-01 in his efforts to obtain a Purple Heart for Joseph B. Kelly. The letter was dated 10 August 2009. Your Staff may not realize that I'm not on the internet as I'm not able to read e-mail messages.

If my answers are too sensitive .... will it's truth. If our President has really awarded the Purple Heart to the soldiers killed at Ft Hood, Texas he is to be commended. Many more soldiers will surely die as the President has changed a murder into a Jihad. Remember that the only thing US Army Major Nidal Malik Hasan has in common with the enemy is that he is a Muslim.

You may phone me at any time during the day at 941-721-6563.

Everyone makes mistakes but awarding the Purple Heart to the soldiers shot or killed by the enemy was not one of them. I'm sure that every Muslim in the world got the message.

       For God and Country,

Ben R. Games, Ph.D
814 Church St Suite #102
Ellenton, FL 34222-2318

Ben R. Games, PhD

Honorable David P. Roe
US Representative TN-01
Washington D.C. 20515-4201   14 December 2009

Ref: Your letter to US Dept of Labor dtd 6 October 2009. (Ref: Kelly)

Honorable David Roe,

Today many people seem to be trying to forget that Iraq and Afghanistan are versions of Vietnam without water. History can not be changed but it can be ignored. You are to be commended for your attempt to help Joseph B. Kelly in his efforts to obtain a Purple Heart for his combat injuries.

As the author of "Confessions of a CIA Interrogator" I based the book upon some of Joe's stories during the period he worked for the US Army as a South Vietnamese Police Advisor. Your first paragraph in the letter for the Department of Labor had an error that most people would never catch.

As an author I only told about what I saw, did, or could verify by two separate sources. Joe was paid as a civil servant (GS-11) of the Department of Labor. The CIA did have an agreement to train civilian employees for the US Army who furnished advisors to the South Vietnam government. Joseph B. Kelly did attended a course at the CIA Blue University where they referred to themselves as Contract Agents and to the actual CIA employees as Jewelers.

I have personally reviewed the medical records of combat injuries that Mr. Joseph B. Kelly received during the firefight to save the civilian employees of the American Embassy. They were classified "secret" but I will testify that the records indicated that Joe was a civilian GS-11 at the time, and his employer was the US Department of Labor.

For God and Country,

PS: I have written my
Congressman Vern
Buchanan, FL-13 requesting he support you.

A Cry for Help

DEFENSE FINANCE AND ACCOUNTING SERVICE

Retired and Annuity Pay

VA RETRO: 1165   January 15, 2010

MAJ BEN R GAMES, USA (Retired)
814 CHURCH ST
SUITE 102
ELLENTON FL 34222-2318

Dear Major GAMES:

This letter is to inform you the Defense Finance and Accounting Service (DFAS) has reviewed your Combat Related Special Compensation (CRSC) / Concurrent Retirement and Disability Pay (CRDP) account.

The Public Laws establishing these entitlements were amended so that retired military members who have previously received, or are currently receiving CRSC and / or CRDP, could have their entitlement(s) recalculated based on retroactive ratings awarded by the Department of Veterans Affairs (DVA).

Our most recent review has determined that your account is current at this time and that these entitlements have been correctly computed for the period of June 2003 through December 2009. A Retiree Account Statement (RAS) will be sent, under separate cover, to confirm the current status of your account.

Should you have any further questions, please contact us at Defense Finance and Accounting Service, US Military Retirement Pay, PO Box 7130, London, KY 40742-7130, or call, toll free, via 1-877-327-4457 (commercial 216-522-6161), Monday through Friday, 8:00 AM to 4:30 PM Eastern Time. You may also send us a toll free fax via 1-800-469-6559.

Sincerely,

Retired and Annuity Pay

PLEASE KEEP A COPY OF THIS LETTER FOR YOUR RECORDS.

Ben R. Games, PhD

Shinn & Company LLC
Mr. Bryon Shinn, CPA
1001 3rd St West Suite 500
Bradenton, FL 34205

15 February 2010

Ref: Information for IRS Form 1041 and Schedules.

Dear Bryon,

I want to thank you for meeting with me at the Edward Jones Investments' office on Tuesday 9 Feb 2010. Pretending to read paragraphs is just one of the things I do. As you learned from our meeting I'm not as sharp as I used too be and need help in understanding tax forms.

Over the years I've developed a method of overcoming some of the aspects of old age and Myasthenia Graves (MG). It consists of asking highly educated individuals to brief me on specific aspects in their fields before attending a conference. This allows me to nod in the right places and to ask questions or make an intelligence comment. Your briefing on the IRS Form 1041 and K1 hopefully will help VFW veterans in the future. Helen (my wife) and I are trying to help our country by giving. Yes, Errol Fletcher knew what I was doing.

Can you believe that in 1982 I would read the captured ledgers of the Drug Cartels' books for the Coast Guard and US Customs Intelligence. Reading math was like watching an adventure story unfold. Some people still don't like the soldiers who work in the shadows but if you ever get to read the story "Death of a Patriot" or Sinking of the Carol "B" you may wish you were there or glad you weren't.

        Thank You Again,

Copy to Edward Jones Investments
Mr. Errol Fletcher, AAMS

Typed but not reread.

MAJ Ben R. Games, Ph.D., USAF (Ret.)
814 CHURCH ST # 102
ELLENTON, FL 34222

A Cry for Help

Honorable Vern Buchanan
Representative FL 13th District
PO Box 4828
Sarasota, FL 34230

1 March 2010

Dear Vern,

I am very sorry that I wasn't able to attend your meeting. I had made arrangements for our Company's Financial Advisor Mr. Errol S. Fletcher, AAMS, to take me to the Town Hall Meeting in Bradenton but at the last minute on Saturday he had to meet with a man who was facing the loss of his retirement funds.

Maybe it's just as well that we weren't able to attend as I do have a habit of expressing myself without worrying about what others may think. As you know one of my disciplines is in Geo-Economics. Today they call it World Economics but the only difference I can see is that seventy years have passed since I studied the subject.

Helen thinks that you would make a good candidate for President but I'm not sure you would want to take on the Federal Reserve Bank. If I remember my history correctly President Jefferson apposed having a Central Bank and President Jackson's actually stopped the JPMorgan Chase Bank from printing money. Senator Aldrich helped organize the Federal Reserve in a secret meeting on Jekyll Island in 1910. After WW-I, Indiana defaulted on all War Bonds issued by the Rothschild's Bank in Paris, so the states' credit was canceled by the Federal Reserve. Today, Indiana is one of the few states that is on the road to a real recovery. Bailouts and stimulus plans are only prolonging the depression but it will definitely strengthen the Federal Reserve's power.

I really want Errol to meet you, and listen to your thoughts on how to stabilize our economy. He is also a manger of Edward Jones Investing Company, and if you would have a few minutes when you are in your Sarasota Office Errol could drive me to Sarasota. If that is not convenient and you are in Bradenton we could meet in his office.

Best Wishes,

DR. BEN R. GAMES PhD.

Ben R. Games, PhD

Mr. Joseph B. Kelly
(CIA Contract Agent RT)
808 Allison Drive
Jonesborough, TN 37659   24 March 2010

Dear Joe,

Sorry about taking so long to answer the question about our reference to the Dark Force in the book "Confession of a CIA Interrogator". I've been busy working on a WW-II nonfiction story called; "The Divine Wind". I reread the book about your work as a CIA Contract Agent, and the newspaper editor was correct; we did refer to how the Dark Force was attacking the United States where the CIA could not legally interfere or provide information to the American citizens.

In the book we referred to God's son Jesus Christ as the commander of the Bright Force and Satan as the leader of the Dark Force. Today the battle is still fought all over the world but the leaders of the Dark Force have convinced the Christens to but political restrictions on the American Soldiers to make the battle field level.

During the Korean War the USAF was not allowed to attack targets in China or Russia. All fighter aircraft had gun cameras and many showed pictures of enemy airfields in China as a kill was made. During the cold war I flew missions over China and Russia but mostly at night so cameras were not used. The plan was to force the US Army to fight on the ground without air support against enemy Forces that out numbered us 5 to 1. In Vietnam it was the same only once again our Generals and the CIA didn't fall into the trap.

Today the enemy has again carried the fight to the American people using terrorists with no known ties to any country. It is true that all Muslims are not terrorists but all terrorists are Muslims. Our elected leader has told the Muslims that our military will not conduct warfare against their faith. The only card that the Black Force hasn't played yet is to introduce the Anti-Christ to lead the fight against Christians.

For God and Country,

Dr. Ben R. Games, PhD
814 Church St # 102
Ellenton, FL 34222

A Cry for Help

Miss Phillippa Wray
American Air Museum Membership Administrator
Imperial War Museum Duxford   20 May 2010

Ref: Your letter dated 10 May 2010. Nonfiction account of women in aero combat, WWII, Korean War, Vietnam War, and the Drug Wars.

Dear Miss Wray,

You may already know that Helen is a glider, singe, multi-engine, and helicopter pilot. What you may not also know is that she has flown as my co-pilot in a B-25 and transport planes during WWII. Once she flew with me in an F-82G as my RO on a combat patrol in 1950, and helicopters in Vietnam with the 1st Cavalry Division (1969). During the secret drug wars in the Caribbean (1980) we lived on Grand Turk while I was the General manager of the Turks & Cacios National Airlines for your country.

One other thing you may find interesting is that Helen, and I will be married 67 years on the 5th of June 2010. The other thing is that she has never been in the military service. Your research department may already know of my flying a L-4 in England in 1965. I have also flown every aircraft in your museum operationally except 4 and that includes the SPAD S-13. I am also rated in balloons and sailplanes.

May Grandmother name was Mary Baker born in London. In 1898 she joined the American Army as a Captain Nurse during the Spanish American War and served in the Philippines Islands.

I am mailing an interview made by the US Pensacola Navy Air Museum and also of our 50th Wedding Anniversary. You may interview us at anytime. There is no charge for our services. We would also consider it an honor if we could give her Majesty a copy of our book called "Santa's Secret". It is a fable about British Island Children that Father Christmas forgot. I can airmail you two copies so it could be read by your research department to be sure it is suitable. One copy may be kept in the museum and one for the gift.

Ben R. Games, Ph.D
814 Church St Suite #102
Ellenton, FL 34222-2318

Ben R. Games, PhD

Editor; VHPA Aviator
5530 Birdcage St, Suite #105
Citrus Heights, CA 95610-7698

(433 words)
28 May 2010

Dear Sir,
I received a note from Ken Fritz without a return address, unsigned, animus.

Helen and I have been trying to remember Ken from when we lived on a firebase in Vietnam. There must be some reason he's upset. If it is about the story "Balls of Fire"; It can't be purchased as I gave it to the VFW Ellenton VFW Post 9226 Building Fund. If it's about the poem "Vietnam Shangri-La"; I gave it to the VHPA. Ken wrote that there were VFW Posts in California if someone wanted to support them. I joined the VFW when Helen and I returned home on the hospital ship the USS Hope after WW-II. I seem to spend a lot of time in hospitals. I have a theory. If the enemy would stop shooting at me Army life would be easy.

I was 57 years old at the time of my last firefight on an island in the Caribbean against the Drug Cartel. The British Navy inserted me and my troops by helicopter. It was out of range of small arms fire; just as the sun was sinking into the sea behind us. This was during the period when America's Policy was not to use American Troops to kill Drug Traffickers.

The British supported me as I knew the enemy but I couldn't carry a firearm. My troopers were from the graduating class of Jamaican police cadets. I carried a cane as I still limped from combat injuries received in Vietnam. The British Navy pilots watched as I led the attack upon the Drug Traffickers waving my cane like a club. My hair is white and my soldiers were black so I really stood out. As we charged toward the enemy they opened fire. Suddenly there was no sound. Everyone had ran out of ammunition at the same time. My soldiers stopped and were just looking at me.

All had passed me half way to the enemy and now here I came waving my stick calling out; "Get the bastards!" My troopers may not be able to shoot but they knew what to do with an empty rife. They followed my lead and used them as clubs. We had one casualty; I ran out of steam. It was kind of like using National Guard soldiers to keep the drug traffickers from the Arizona police. When you don't have police powers a M-16 makes a good club. Just follow the VFW veterans waving their canes for they know the enemy.

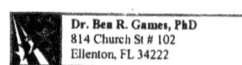

Dr. Ben R. Games, PhD
814 Church St # 102
Ellenton, FL 34222

A Cry for Help

Camp Grayling Officers' Club Fund
www.cgfund.org

29 August 2010

Dear Ben,

    First I would like to thank you for your continued support to our Camp Grayling O'Club Endowment Fund. As you are aware this summer the Fund Development Committee hosted a Donor Recognition Luncheon. We had a nice turn out of 50 donors and after I reviewed our situation we cut a special cake that was decorated with the fund's total of $154,480. That is a record high! This new high would not have been possible without consistent donors such as your self! I have enclosed a copy of the information sheets I handed out during the luncheon.

    The second thing I wanted to talk to you about is our fall "Award Winning" newsletter. (No, I have not created the award that we've won yet but I am closer then last year ☺). At our Fund Development meeting this summer the Committee recommended that the newsletter feature you in the annual "Portrait of a Donor" column. It was a unanimous decision!

    So to help me fashion the story I need 3 things from you. 1. A copy of your current biography. 2. A sentence or two why you support our growing Endowment Fund for the O'Club's preservation. 3. A photo that you would like used in the column. A "mug" shot would be good.

    After I am finished with the story I will send you a copy before we go to press. I have the information on Fideli Publishing Inc. and I will let the readers know how to contact them for information on the books you have written.

    I was over at Ft. Custer the other day and they were pleased to have the Distinguished Flying Cross framed document to place in their growing museum.

    Again, thanks for your continued financial support and your help on the Portrait of a Donor column

    Jackie says hello and thank you. She has enjoyed all of your books.

BG Warren J. Lawrence (Ret)
15740 Poplar Lane
Vicksburg, MI 49097
269-649-0340

Ben R. Games, PhD

BG Warren J. Lawrence
15740 Poplar Lane
Vicksburg, MI 49097   10 September 2010

Dear Warren,

1. Current biography? When I started to write my biography it was to be three (3) books named my "Guardian Angel", "Without Prejudice", and "Senior Pilot." That was the plan until I realized that some other writer would have to finish "Senior Pilot" when I could no longer toe the line. In February this year I started writing the 24th story of my autobiography named "FUUJIN" (the Okinawa God of Wind).

a. Answer; I have enclosed one story called "A Terrorist Mirror" and a copy of the CD Distinguished Flying Cross (10 minutes). Mr. Vern Buchanan is our FL 13th Representative (R), and was a fighter pilot for the MIANG but Vern has never told me if he approves of President Lincoln's suggestion.

2. Question; Why do we support the Endowment Fund? When the Base Chapel was under construction Lt/General Snipkie asked for donations. Helen and I gave $500.00 the very next day for one of the new classrooms. There was never a question about giving to the Officers Club Endowment Fund when you asked us to help. It was only how much should we donate.

a. Answer; Helen and I have a system of trying to help in a way that people can respect us for who we are and not for what we give. The Endowment Fund does this. The Base Chapel accepted $500.00 dollars so that is the amount of our gift. It's a gift that keeps on giving. We quickly learned in the MI Army National Guard no soldier stands alone.

3. Question; Picture of donor?

a. If you can only use one person please use Helen's picture. If you need advice please ask Jackie. Helen flew in transports and once as my co-pilot in a B-25 during WW-II. She flew on a combat patrol as my F-82G Radar operator during the Korean War, and combat in Vietnam. She as the 86th women in the World to fly helicopters. Helen completed combat survival training with the Army Nurses at Ft Rucker in 1969.

Ben R. Games

Ben R. Games, Ph.D
814 Church St Suite #102
Ellenton, FL 34222-2318

A Cry for Help

Bradenton VA Clinic
Suite #101
5520 St Rd 64 E.
Bradenton, FL 34208

1 November 2010

To: Dr. James A. Carnahan. MD

Ref: Annual Physical for Ben R. Games, PhD. VA File #Ci5-227-804.

Dear James,

I had written some notes concerning items that were causing me problems. One; was remembering where I had put things on my desk, names, and even the actual date of my physical. During the physical you asked how many time I had to get up at night. I think I told you three or four times, but I'm not sure. I had stopped drinking water in the late afternoon and that seemed to help. The Lab technician informed me that now they were having problems finding enough blood for testing the Coumadin. Today I drank water and they had no trouble finding blood. Is this a dammed if I do and dammed if I don't things?

My second problem is the pain in my back. I have no problem remembering that it was on the 8th November 1969 at 1230 hours. Even today I can remember the date and time the pain started. It happened at LZ Vivian, Vietnam, the instant my helicopter hit the ground after falling 800 feet in a ball of fire. Today the pain has increased to where my back brace is not enough. Once a long time ago the VA orthopedics doctors told me that I had to get out of my wheelchair. My question is can I take something for pain or is it another dammed if I do and dammed if I don't things?

Thanks

DR. BEN R. GAMES PhD.

Ben R. Games, PhD

DEPARTMENT OF THE ARMY
U.S. ARMY HUMAN RESOURCES COMMAND
1600 SPEARHEAD DIVISION AVENUE
FORT KNOX, KY 40122

OCT 1 9 2010

Awards and Decorations Branch

Dr. Ben R. Games, Ph.D
814 Church Street, Suite 102
Ellenton, Florida 34222-2318

Dear Dr. Games:

  Thank you for your recent letter to President Barack H. Obama concerning your desire to have your DD Form 214 (Report of Separation) updated to include the Vietnam Wound Medal. Due to mail screening procedures, we have only recently received your letter. We appreciate your patience in awaiting this response.

  The Vietnam Wound Medal is not a Department of the Army award. It is not authorized for wear by U.S. Service Members and cannot be added to your DD Form 214.

  Thank you for your service to our Nation.

         Sincerely,

         Stewart L. Stephenson, Jr.
         Lieutenant Colonel, U.S. Army
         Chief, Awards and Decorations Branch

Printed on Recycled Paper

A Cry for Help

3 November 2010
Ben

Departmen of the Army	Chief of
Human Resources Command	Awards & Decoration Branch
1600 Spearhead Division Avenue	Lieutenant Colonel
Fort Knox, KY 40122	Stewart L. Stephenson, Jr.

Ref: Your Letter dated 19 Oct 2010; subject, answer for President Obama.

Dear Stewart,

I am aware that you may not have read the letter our Commander-in-chief sent to your office. You may also know Lt/Colonel Sylvia A. Bennett who wrote informing me that the men I recommended for the Purple Heart and myself were not on the Historical Casualty List. In my research for the story "A Terrorist Mirror" I was never able to verify that there were actually two lists for individuals wounded or killed in the Vietnam War. She also recommended that I should use the courts and sue the Army.

I followed her advice but possibly not in the way she intended. My DD214 was corrected to allow the wearing of the Vietnam CAMPAIGN MEDAL W/1960 device, Republic of Vietnam Gallantry Cross w/Palm Unit Citation, and Republic of Vietnam Civil Actions Medal of Honor. The Veterans Administration also conducted a De Novo Review of medical evidence on record for award of the DFC (heroism) and other combat injures. The Court wrote; based upon this evidence Major Games is a combat Veteran and the provisions of 38 CFR 3.304 (d) apply.

My letter to the President did not request any changes to my DD214. I believe that President Obama sent you this letter to observe protocol and allow the Army to recognize their own. If you need my research records of Dave Walker or Joseph Kelly please contact my publisher.

For GOD and Country,

Send Copy to Joe Kelly
David Walker
Ben

Ben R James

Maj Ben R Games Ph D
814 Church St # 102
Ellenton FL 34222-2318

Ben R. Games, PhD

22 Nov 10

To Major Ben Games

This is the way I handled my dead and wounded men. I sent my wounded men to american hospital under guard no one could talk to them, I also gave them Vietnam reward for wounds received and when they got killed I put the first nail in the coffin and I placed a flag over the coffin. I also shinked the cracks in the coffin out of respect as well as a gun volley. For the americans I placed a medal as well as varified that they belong to me. I then paid the wife 1 year pay for her husband death and flew them back to their home by air America aircraft.

I also had authority to promote and fire any men under my command as directed by Lt General Timmes.

Joseph B Kelly
CIA Field Officer
Vietnam

A Cry for Help

Robert M. Silmser
4701 Bear Claw Ct
Valrico, FL 33594   21 November 2009

Ref: Your layout for the Plaque at Tampa's Veterans Park.

Dear Bob,

It was a good layout and was just what I needed.

Please find enclosed the corrected copies. There were three spelling errors, and they were more than likely from my computer. I've found the spell check program will sometimes even change a word after a letter has been posted.

I deleted the CH-47 from my son's combat helicopter flying in Vietnam as he only flew in my Chinook on Christmas day (1969) to LZ Burt. The Red Hat on the LZ radio called asking if we could help the soldiers get to Christmas dinner while the food was still hot. All I had to do was pick up a sling load from the log pad and move it a half-mile to a trench that had been dug in a cleared area. I told Jon over the intercom that he could lay on the deck next to the center hatch with the flight engineer to watch me work.

There was a rope fastened to a fiber donut that one of the soldiers attached to the Chinook's hook. I lifted the load slowly while asking what the load was. The flight engineer called over the intercom that the load was a hundred dead North Vietnamese soldiers that were tied to the rope. It seems that the LZ had been attacked on Christmas Eve, and the Battalion Commander had told the soldiers that no one could eat until the bodies had been buried.

I am not sure this is really combat but then again it may be.

I have one other small problem and that is with the Poem "Shangri-La Vietnam". I wrote it for all Vietnam Helicopter Pilots, and donated to the VHPA. I do not believe it would be fitting or proper to use it as a personal poem. It maybe that the pilots do not like it, and if that is true then it should not be used. You may even ask everyone to cast a vote on its use and donate a dollar for each vote. This way it may help the museum project even if the poem stinks.

                    Good Luck,

                                        DR. BEN R. GAMES PhD.

Ben R. Games, PhD

PACIFIC AVIATION MUSEUM — PEARL HARBOR
FORD ISLAND, HAWAII

20427

ADM Ronald J. Hays, USN (Ret.)
Chairman

HONORARY CHAIRMAN
President George H. W. Bush

BOARD OF DIRECTORS

CHAIRMAN
ADM Ronald J. Hays, USN (Ret.)

PRESIDENT
Clinton R. Churchill

EXECUTIVE VICE PRESIDENT
ADM R. J. "Zap" Zlatoper, USN (Ret.)

VICE PRESIDENTS
Charles K. Cotton
MG Edward V. Richardson, USAF (Ret.)
Darrell G. Welch, Jr.

VICE PRESIDENT AND LEGAL COUNSEL
Peter Starn

SECRETARY
Richard M. May, Jr.

TREASURER
Harvey Gray

ASSISTANT TREASURER
Michael L. Olsen

DIRECTORS
Kenneth R. Bailey
Carolyn Berry
Aileen Blanc
VADM Michael Bowman, USN (Ret.)
Henry P. Bruckner
BrigGen Benjamin Cassiday, USAF (Ret.)
RADM Ken Fisher, USN (Ret.)
Dennis Fitzgerald
Charles L. Goodwin
LtGen Earl Hailston, USMC (Ret.)
Lisa Hamilton
Jim Hickerson
BrigGen Dwight M. Kealoha, USAF (Ret.)
Thomas S. Kosasa, MD
Thomas E. Lawrence
Ruth Limtiaco
BrigGen Frances Mossman, USAF (Ret.)
Donn Parent
James K. Schuler
William Shankel, MD
John T. Sterling
Edward E. Swofford
Bell Ward
Kenneth D. Wiecking

EXECUTIVE DIRECTOR
Kenneth H. DeHoff, Jr.

ADVISORY BOARD
ADM Stanley R. Arthur, USN (Ret.)
Gerald Coffee
Gen John K. Davis, USMC (Ret.)
Superintendent Paul DePrey, NPS
BGen Jerome Hagen, USMC (Ret.)
ADM Thomas B. Hayward, USN (Ret.)
VADM Gerald H. Hoewing, USN (Ret.)
R. A. "Bob" Hoover
VADM William D. Houser, USN (Ret.)
Senator Daniel K. Inouye
Dr. Timothy Keck
Gen John Lorber, USAF (Ret.)
Senator John McCain, III
Gen Merrill A. McPeak, USAF (Ret.)
Jim Nabors
BrigGen Chuck Yeager, USAF (Ret.)

December 3, 2010

Helen M. Games Mba
814 Church St. Ste. 102
Ellenton, FL 34222-2318

Dear Helen:

I believe you recently received a letter under my signature seeking your support of Pacific Aviation Museum Pearl Harbor but which, unfortunately, contained reference to the detention of Japanese-Americans during WWII.

While the letter was sent by our direct mail service under my signature, through an internal museum administrative blunder that violated policy, the letter was not reviewed by me or the executive staff before it was distributed.

We deeply apologize for any consternation that the letter has caused. It does not reflect our philosophy nor feelings about the history of Japanese-Americans during WWII. We are embarrassed that letter went out but wanted to now communicate the museum's disavowal of the comments made in the letter.

Our mission is simple: To develop and maintain an internationally recognized aviation museum on historic Ford Island that educates young and old alike, honors aviators and their support personnel who defended freedom in the Pacific Region, and preserves Pacific aviation history.

Helen, we thank you for your understanding and wish you a very happy holiday season.

Very truly yours,

Ronald J Hays

ADM Ronald J. Hays, USN (Ret.)
Chairman

Mailed and the Purns word 12-21-2010 Ben

Hangar 37, Ford Island · 319 Lexington Blvd, Honolulu, HI 96818 · tel (808) 441-1000 · fax (808) 441-1019
e-mail: info@pacificaviationmuseum.org · www.pacificaviationmuseum.org

A Cry for Help

Chairman Adm. Ronald J. Hays
Hanger 37, Ford Island
319 Lexington Blvd
Honolulu, HI   96818   21 December 2010

Dear Ronald,

I received you letter concerning; detention of Japanese-Americans during WW-II. I remember the Japanese-American Camp I visited was located near Wellington, Arizona next to Highway 238 in 1942. The camp buildings were unpainted wooden buildings surrounded by barbed wire. The family apartments were two 10'X10' rooms, and the showers with toilets attached were in separate buildings. Many of their farms were stolen by Politicos.

Later I recruited Nisei soldiers to work in a team that was hunting Japanese war-crime criminals in the Philippines, Okinawa, and Japan. I also visited the prisoner of war camps that held Americans and believe me the ones in Arizona were pure luxury. One criminal we hunted was a Japanese doctor who would infect prisoners with a disease and then perform an autopsy while they were still alive. In 1945 we were also hunting for the Politico in the United States who was trying to purchase the doctor's notes. It lead back to the State Department and no charges were filed.

It appears that you are being used by some Politico who maybe setting the stage for something big. Its happened to me a few times and I never liked it, but we both have the strongest ally (truth) in the world on our side. Remember; History is a window that looks into the future. Politicos try to change history everyday but it can not be done. Today your Museum is in great danger for we now have a figure in our government called the regulatory czar. This individual is not an elected figure, and under no laws in our constitution. He rejects the rule that "Congress shall make no law abridging the freedom of speech." Because the Politicos in our government are men and not angels we must not allow them the kind of power this regulatory czar desires and claims.

May I suggest that you should not spend the Museum's money or time worrying about the Japanese. To learn more you can read "The Divine Wind" by Ben R. Games, PhD.

DR. BEN R. GAMES PhD.

Ben R. Games, PhD

INTRODUCTION

Vietnam Shangri-la was written as Helen and I sat beside the swimming pool at the Ashia Hotel in Bangkok, Thailand, drinking iced tea and talking as husbands and wives do the world over. We had just returned from visiting our son Ben Jr. (Bud) who was in the US Navy at Da Nang, Vietnam. Helen was telling me she had nothing to do while I was having all the fun flying for the Thai Marine Police.

As a good husband, I was trying to help. I suggested that she keep notes on our trips and write stories about them. Her argument was that no one would want to read about us sitting in a CIA airline plane in Saigon for two hours waiting for fighterbombers to take of. To prove that some readers might be interested, I borrowed a typewriter and wrote *Vietnam Shangri-la* in 1967. The only writer's liberty I took was that I compressed time. Weeks became hours and for the reader, the long periods of boredom just disappeared. I didn't give the name of the branch of service or rank of the men we talked to. I wanted the reader to feel as if he or she knew how a son or husband was living and fighting. I mailed the story to a *Moblehome*

Magazine, and we forgot about it. The story was printed in countries all over the world and in newspapers everywhere.

Actually Helen is a hands-on manager and is in charge of the daily operations of our business. She travels with me and keeps track of money flows, managers, represents us at board meetings, and briefs me on business matters. She does this while raising our two sons and keeping our house, no matter where we are living. I believe that she does this without even thinking about the difficulties of the job. I take her on some flights flying fighters and helicopters but never on bombing missions. She doesn't like dropping bombs. I do this to impress her with my work, but wives think they can do it better, and maybe some times they can.

In our family, my job is to be the food gatherer and to protect the family. Sometimes, I really have to find the food and fight to protect them. It isn't about having a job, but more about the raw living of having to hunt for something to eat and a shelter to keep the rain off that I find exciting.

We are Christians and members of the LDS church. I know there is only one God, and if he has promised the enemy that when they die they will have 72 virgins then I know that when we meet in the hereafter they will be happy because I have helped them get there. If not, they will be so busy that they won't notice me. I do pray that Helen will have a higher level in heaven than me so she will know that I'm not having more fun. I know she will still keep my house in order wherever we are. I will continue to defend and protect her. Hopefully I will not have to hunt for food.

My priorities have always been "For God and Country."

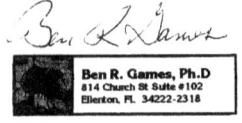

A Cry for Help

Honorable Vern Buchanan
1516 Longworth House Office Building
Washington D.C. 20515   17 February 2009

Dear Vern,

Thanks for your personal letter dtd 2 February 2009. My answer to your question is that the two US Border Guards should have been paid a bonus, given a medal, and promoted. In 1980 before the military had police powers I was sent to the Caribbean to stop drugs from being transported on TCNA (Nation Airline) planes.

Soon after I arrived a convicted drug smuggler and murder was captured by the police, and I was asked to transport him to the court on another island. I had the man placed in leg irons with hands fastened behind his back. Then I used duck tape to hold the trigger back on my young native policemen's shotgun. The prisoner was seated in the back facing forward and strapped in with duck tape facing the policeman. Next the duck tape was used to hold the shotgun's barrel into his mouth; yes it was loaded. The flight was only going to take an hour but from the look on the prisoner and guard's face they must both have thought it was going to be forever. Just before take off I pulled back the hammer of the policeman's weapon and told him that if he let go he would have to clean the plane.

There was really no danger to the aircraft as we never flew higher than 2000 feet, and there were no passengers. I was not in court for the hearing but the Judge told the Commissioner of Police that the prisoner had not killed any of their people and only five Americans in the United States. The Americans had lost the prisoner once, and he was really their problem. The Judge then told the court that Americans did not like terrorists or drug smugglers, and the Commissioner should remember this the next time he needed prisoners moved. The Judge fined the prisoner one hundred thousand dollars, and three days later the drug cartel raided the prison to release him.

I have always liked duck tape and in Vietnam it was used to patch the bullet holes in my Chinook. Since then I've found many other uses for the sticky stuff.

         For God and Country,

                           DR. BEN R. GAMES PhD.

Ben R. Games, PhD

TRANSPORTATION AND
INFRASTRUCTURE COMMITTEE
SUBCOMMITTEE ON HIGHWAYS AND TRANSIT
SUBCOMMITTEE ON AVIATION

VETERANS' AFFAIRS COMMITTEE

SMALL BUSINESS COMMITTEE
SUBCOMMITTEE ON FINANCE AND TAX
SUBCOMMITTEE ON REGULATIONS,
HEALTHCARE AND TRADE

CONGRESSMAN VERN BUCHANAN
HOUSE OF REPRESENTATIVES
THIRTEENTH DISTRICT, FLORIDA

February 2, 2009

Dr. Ben R. Games
814 Church Street
#102
Ellenton, FL 34222-2318

Dear Dr. Games:

Knowing of your opposition to illegal immigration, I wanted to make sure you knew that two U.S. Border Patrol agents convicted of shooting a Mexican drug smuggler have had their sentences commuted by President George W. Bush.

Although this was not the full pardon that I supported, it will result in the agents being freed from prison within the next few weeks.

Agents Ignacio Ramos and Jose Alonso Compean were convicted of shooting an admitted drug smuggler in 2005, as he fled across the Rio Grande River back into Mexico. Prosecutors alleged the agents failed to report the shooting and tampered with evidence. Agent Ramos was sentenced to 11 years in prison, while Agent Compean was sentenced to 12 years.

I supported a congressional pardon (H.R. 563) for both agents because they were doing their job of guarding our border, and they were unfairly prosecuted and imprisoned. The bill I supported also called for the Department of Homeland Security to review the rules of engagement used by Border Patrol personnel in order to prevent miscarriages of justice like this from happening again.

Please let me know your opinion on this matter. Email my legislative staffer who handles immigration policy, Mr. Spencer Bell, at spencer.bell@mail.house.gov and tell him if you think the President took the proper action by commuting Ramos and Compean's sentences.

As always, should you have any further questions or concerns, please do not hesitate to contact me.

Sincerely,

Vern Buchanan
Member of Congress

This mailing was prepared, published, and mailed at taxpayer expense.

1516 LONGWORTH HOUSE OFFICE BUILDING WASHINGTON, DC 20515 (202) 225-5015 FAX: (202) 226-0828	235 NORTH ORANGE AVENUE SUITE 201 SARASOTA, FL 34236 (941) 951-6643 FAX: (941) 951-2972	1001 THIRD AVENUE WEST SUITE 380 BRADENTON, FL 34205 (941) 747-9081 FAX: (941) 749-5310

www.buchanan.house.gov

A Cry for Help

VA Benefit Details

SERVICE-CONNECTED DISABILITY: If yes, the Veteran is receiving VA benefits for a condition incurred during or aggravated by military service.

COMBINED SERVICE-CONNECTED EVALUATION: The Veteran's combined evaluation for all conditions determined to be service-connected.

CURRENT MONTHLY AWARD AMOUNT: The monetary benefit paid to Veterans and survivors who are receiving benefits under a VA program.

NON-SERVICE-CONNECTED PENSION: Benefit for non-service connected Veteran's who meet specific criteria, which include wartime service, minimum length of service, and income restrictions. If a Veteran is eligible for service-connected benefits and pension benefits, VA will pay the higher benefit.

INDIVIDUAL UNEMPLOYABILITY (IU): Veteran is receiving payment at the 100 percent rate, even though the combined service connected evaluation is not 100 percent. The Veteran's service-connected conditions cause him/her to be unable to obtain or maintain substantially gainful employment because of the Veteran's service-connected conditions. These Veterans must periodically certify continued unemployability, but if there is no scheduled future reduction or medical examination required, they may be considered by some states to be permanently and totally disabled.

PERMANENT AND TOTAL (P&T) DISABILITY: Veteran is considered by VA to be totally and permanently disabled because of his/her service-connected conditions.

FUTURE EXAMINATION: If this line appears on the letter, the Veteran is scheduled for a follow-up medical examination on the date shown, to determine the current level of disability.

FUTURE REDUCTION: If this line appears on the letter, the Veteran is currently receiving temporary disability benefits. On the date shown, the Veteran's temporary disability period will expire, and the combined service-connected evaluation will be reduced.

SPECIAL MONTHLY COMPENSATION: If yes, the Veteran is service-connected for loss of or loss of use of a limb, or is totally blind in or missing at least one eye.

SPECIALLY ADAPTED HOUSING and/or SPECIAL HOME ADAPTATION GRANT: Grants provided by VA to service-connected veterans and service members to help build a new specially adapted house, to adapt a home they already own, or buy a house and modify it to meet their disability-related requirements.

Wartime Service Periods

Mexican Border Period: May 9, 1916, through April 5, 1917, for veterans who served in Mexico, on its borders or in adjacent waters.

World War I: April 6, 1917, through Nov. 11, 1918; for veterans who served in Russia, April 6, 1917, through April 1, 1920; extended through July 1, 1921, for veterans who had at least one day of service between April 6, 1917, and Nov. 11, 1918.

World War II: Dec. 7, 1941, through Dec. 31, 1946.

Korean War: June 27, 1950, through Jan. 31, 1955.

Vietnam War: Aug. 5, 1964 (Feb. 28, 1961, for veterans who served "in country" before Aug. 5, 1964), through May 7, 1975.

Gulf War: Aug. 2, 1990, through a date to be set by law or Presidential Proclamation.

Ben R. Games, PhD

Department of Veterans Affairs
Congressional Office
B-328 Rayburn House Office Building
US House of Representative   20 September 2005
Washington, DC 20515

Ref: Letter dated 15 Sept. 2005 from Secretary of Defense, Health Affairs,
 VA File # 15 227 804, Games, Ben R. St Petersburg Regional Office.

Dear Sirs;

Sorry, it may be my age or Myasthenia Gravis, but I can not remember the letter that I wrote to the Secretary of Defense Health Affairs on the 1st of June 2005. I have written many letters in support of the Veterans Administration asking for someone to assist them and our citizen soldiers. On the 17 December 2004 I received a letter from the VA informing me about a problem with their computer records. I have been attempting to help them by asking for everyone to assist them. Maybe you know someone.

On the 2 December 2004 the US Army Physical Disability Agency first requested information from the VA St Petersburg Regional Office the reasons for issuing VA non-combat disability codes #7706, 7346, and 5003 for my combat injuries. They also requested medical records and supporting documents for these non-combat codes.

It makes me unhappy when someone is shooting at me but I really get mad when I'm told the computer said it didn't happen. If someone with over 27 years active duty and my documented combat record with awards for heroism can have this happen just think of the citizen soldier injured fighting today. When he or she is my age will some computer terrorist change the records to show they weren't injured in combat because a battle had been won or indicate they weren't really there?

A VA letter 9/6/05 stated that my active duty has been verified except for the period of service 10/01/1962 to 07/01/1973. The VA has pictures, a Army Times article, copy of awards for heroism, and my retirement DD214 yet its not enough. Maybe it's just that I served my country longer than most.

    Sincerely;

          DR. BEN R. GAMES PhD.

A Cry for Help

Honorable Senator John McCain OPEN LETTER
Senate Office Building
Washington, DC, 20510   4 August 2008

Ref: How the World Works.

Dear John,

Only someone who knew the "Rodent", or was a resident of the Hon Lo Prison can truly understand that the Dark Force never gives up.

The Iraq War is the Vietnam War without water.

The World is entering a Geo-Feudal Age. Instead of Presidents and Kings there are CEO's. Instead of Senators & Representatives there are committees, and boards reporting to Department Secretaries. Instead of patriots following their flag there will be mega geo-companies without national boundaries. Instead of citizens there will be stockholders with loyalty only to the company.

The World Shed Tears.

All American Service men and women may someday wear the same uniform. Not unlike Vietnam. Iraq may also be policed by a Mega Geo-Company paid for by the oil sold to American citizens. No need for a US Navy, USAF, or a standing US Army in Iraq. Loyalties and Countries can be bought and sold on the World Stock Exchanges. Best of all only the Iraq people, the police, and the terrorist would die. Iraq could forget about freedom, and Americans wouldn't have to think at all.

America's Volunteer Navy.

One sure way to slow down volunteer enlistments is to issue Vouchers for their healthcare. Give every American who is a coward, illegal alien, or terrorist the same benefits as an American Patriot. Save money by having a private corporation to oversee the issuing of Health Vouchers which should stop congress from voting on Veterans Administration funding.

DR. BEN R. GAMES PhD.

SHANGRI-LA VIETNAM

by Ben R. Games, PhD

A long time ago in a land far, far away young men flitted around trees and villages. They flew over rice paddies and amongst rubber plantations. In the jungle they were like humming birds feeding on flowers. Shangri-la you are here.

The sun was bright and the air warm. Flowers brightened the dark green grass, and the land was peaceful. Hats of woven grass protected the men and women working in rice paddies while the young men watched from the sky. In the villages men in white silk shirts and dark trousers walked with women wearing white silk pajama pants under split silk dresses with the bright colors of a rainbow. The picture brought thoughts of love and home to the young men flying their screaming birds. Shangri-la you are here.

A Cry for Help

Young men of yesterday flitted around the towns and fields with the sound of the blades going "Wop, Wop". Voices in their ears from LZs were calling, "Come to me! Come to me!" It was like flowers calling to Bees, "Pick me! Pick me!" Shangri-la you are here.

Fly like a bird close to mother earth, peek around a building, look over a wall, stop and back up or turn around. Never having to pay for fuel. Shangri-la you are here.

Suddenly a dark wall appears creeping steadily across the land. The fields are empty. The noise of children and bright clothing are gone from the towns. A flash of light, the darkness, the sound of thunder or is it the guns. It's all the same as the young men fly to the battle as moths go to a flame. Many are consumed. Wherever the young men touch the wall of hate and fear, hope springs forth. Shangri-la where have you gone?

Ben R. Games, PhD

Spirit Guards From Sunset To Sunrise
Games Home Filled With

The Elkhart Truth
FOR TODAY'S *Woman*

TUESDAY, JUNE 26, 1973

By MARCIA FULMER
Truth Women's Reporter

"We enjoy!"
In these two words, Mrs. Ben (Helen) Games expresses the attitude she and her husband share towards life.

A visit to their home near Union takes you through room after room filled with objects collected during years of travel around the world... each with its own special story and memories.

High On Hill

The house itself sits high on a wooded hill, away from the busy highway. "We come here between trips," Mrs. Games laughs, "when we want to get away and relax."

Wild birds and animals gather at a feeding area off the newly-built recreation room, well aware that none will be allowed to go hungry during the cold winter months.

A pair of Thai Fu dogs, guardians of the home, flank the front entrance. Inside, Spanish silver goblets, German beer steins and Dutch wooden shoes serve as reminders of the couple's many visits abroad.

The master bedroom contains Mrs. Games' collection of pigeon blood lacquer vases, an ornate Japanese box used for sewing by her husband's grandmother, and several Japanese statues.

Frames Cost More

One in particular is a family favorite. Affectionately dubbed "George," the china figure depicts a seated male with a greatly exaggerated forehead and long earlobes. These two features, according to Mrs. Games, denote great wisdom.

Also in the bedroom hang three cloth temple rubbings from Thailand. To create them, the bare material was rubbed over carvings in a temple, then painted and gilded to complete the scene.

To illustrate the relative monetary cost of souvenirs in Asia, Mrs. Games notes ruefully, "The frames

A Cry for Help

Souvenirs Of Faraway Sites

SPIRIT HOUSE — In a wooded setting outside her Union home, Mrs. Ben Games places a joss stick before a Thai spirit house. Natives of Thailand believe the ornate, temple-like structure to be the home of a guardian spirit and, in Bangkok, Mrs. Games reports "Every family has one." The metal frame and peaked fiberglass roof were added to protect it from the elements.

AUTHORS PERSONAL INFORMATION

Ben R. Games, PhD, Major, CW-4, TCNA-6, flew bombers and night fighters during WWII. Then Jet Fighters for the USAF during the Korean War, and helicopters in Vietnam for the 1st Cavalry Division. He is a member of the North American Mach Busters Club and of the Distinguished Flying Cross Society with 737 recorded combat hours. After 35 years he retired from military flying in 1978 and later became the manager of the Turks & Caicos National Airline.

The author served in Vietnam as a pilot with the 228 Aviation Battalion, Company B, and "E" Battery 82nd Artillery in the 1st Cavalry Division. He is also a life member of Army Aviation Class 43K, 1st Cavalry Division Association, MOAA, USAF Association, VHPA, DFC Society, National Guard Association of the US, Camp Grayling Officers Club, VFW, American Legion, and the DAV.

During his military service Ben was awarded the Distinguished Flying Cross for Heroism, Bronze Star, 13 Air Medals, Army Commendation Medal with "V" Device, National Defense Service Medal w/3 Bronze Service Stars, MI Medals of Valor w/Oak leaf cluster, two Legion of Merit. Vietnam Campaign Medal w/1960 device, Republic of Vietnam Gallantry Cross w/Palm Unit Citation, and Republic of Vietnam Civil Actions Medal of Honor with First Class Unit Citation.

During the past fifty years stories of his adventures have been read by people around the world. They range from a child's Christmas story, biographical adventures, to science fiction.

BOOKS WRITTEN; www.FideliPublishing.com

Fideli Publishing, Inc.
SALES

Ben R. Games, PhD; all the author's books may be ordered through:

Fideli Publishing Inc.
119 W. Morgan St.
Martinsville, IN 46151

Phone: (888) 343-3542 or Fax (765) 537-2971

(Phone for costs of paperback books & Wholesale Prices.)

www.FideliPublishing.com

MY GUARDIAN ANGEL is about flying during WWII & Korea. All pilots need a Guardian Angel and this was especially true in these stories. Autobiography.

WITHOUT PREJUDICE is an autobiography of an Army Aviator during the Vietnam War. He is married to a beautiful lady, and they live on a Fire Base called Bearcat. The story is about a Chinook Helicopter named the "City of Elkhart" that was destroyed in a fire fight at LZ Vivian.

POWERED PARACHUTE ZONE is a Coffee Table Picture Book about flying powered parachutes from farmers fields. It's all about being free.

SANTA'S SECRET is woven from the fabric of the author's imagination. The people are real, and they really helped Santa as told in the fable. The story is about how Santa Claus forgot the children of the Turks and Caicos Islands, BWI. This is a Christmas Story for everyone.

BEYOND is a science fiction story about Roswell, New Mexico and the astronauts from Zoran. It tells how they came to earth looking for help in their war against the Altairons, and how an American pilot became one of their Battle Captains. This store is not for the weak at heart.

MONTANA'S VACATION is a true story of a black Labrador Retriever trained as a Guide Dog who is taking his Companion on a vacation cruise in the Caribbean. The story is being told by Montana, and it's all about his adventures on the Holland American Lines Cruise Ships, and how he helps his Companion find the poop deck.

SINKING OF THE CAROL "B" is a semi-autobiographic story told by "Montana" a black Labrador Retriever Guide Dog,. It's about fighting in the Turks & Caicos Islands Drug War, and forming a secret intelligent organization with a code that has never been broken.

DEATH OF A PATRIOT is a semi-biographic story told by "Montana" a black Labrador Retriever. It tells about how JAGS the Chief Minister of the Turks and Caicos Islands was assassinated in the secret drug war that saved his country from the drug cartels.

ADVENTURES OF BENNY BOB are autobiographic stories with pictures of the author's life in the wild, wild, West during the great depression and the building of Hoover Dam. There are also stories and poems written by members of the Games Clan with a paragraph about the author's relationship to Ben and Helen. It's about how a young man developed into a warrior during the great depression.

CONFESSION OF A CIA INTERROGATOR is a nonfiction adventure story of a CIA Contract Agent in Vietnam. The Communist had a plan to trap the US Army in the Saigon area and destroy it when the Paris Pease Accord was signed. Bill Colby, CIA OIC, also had a plan to destroy all Communist VC along the route to Saigon and delay the North Vietnamese for two week to allow the US Army to escape the trap. Gilbert H. Moriggia, CIA Agent was Colby's man in the field.

SOLO Class 90Z is the last Class Book of Army Primary Class Book of 43K at Fort Stockton, Texas during WWII. It is a true story with Ray C. Murry, 43J editor, and the author Ben R. Games, 43J & 43K members of the GIBBS FIELD ALUMNI ASSOCIATION 20 October 1990.

JIHAD VIETNAM by Ben R. Games, PhD is a nonfiction book of the CIA's secret war within a war to save the United States from the Dark Forces. The American forces used a body count of enemy soldiers to prove their success at winning a battle. The Dark Forces counted everyone, women, children, and civilians as well as military soldiers killed and they won. After the Americans signed the Paris Peace Accord giving South Vietnam to the Dark Forces history records that the killing really started. 1.7 million Cambodians were executed, over 1 million Laos people were killed, and 25% of South Vietnamese were killed or had to leave their homeland.

GALAXY SLAVES is a Science Fiction novel and is a sequel to BEYOND. It is based on true facts known about the universe today, and tells how robots have developed into self thinking machines. It is also about how humans and robots learned to work together to save the human race. After the last great battle to prevent humans from being raised like cattle to be eaten the robots went looking for God to ask if they could become a host for His souls.

BALLS OF FIRE is a semi-biographic and nonfiction account of a Chinook CH-47 helicopter assigned to "B" Company 228th Av Bn, 1st Cavalry Division, Vietnam. It tells how it got the name "City of Elkhart" and how it arrived in Vietnam. It also tells about the artillery raids into Cambodia and the Snatch and Grab kidnapping of Viet Cong for interrogation by

CIA Contract Agents. The story is also about its crew and how it liked flying Helen the wife of its Aircraft Commander.

THE TERRORIST MIRROR is a nonfiction semi-biographical tale about a military mission in Vietnam where Helen and Gentle Ben took a convoy through a free fire zone from Bear Cat to Phouc Vinh. It was the bait for a trap to entice a North Vietnamese Tank Battalion to come out of hiding. It soon became a race between the enemy, and 1st Cavalry Tanks. The bait was a platoon of Thai soldiers, one US Army tank, one armed personnel vehicle, a 2½ ton truck, and a OH-6 Loach helicopter.

THE BANGKOK DROP is a nonfiction semi-biography. It's about researching targets for B-52 bombers. The author traveled with a group of school children to visit a Cambodian Buddhist Temple. During the visit he would leave the Temple and seek out factories building antiaircraft guns. After returning to Bangkok, Thailand the location of targets would be placed into a CIA Drop Box.

WASPs OF WWII is a nonfiction story of women pilots training at Avenger Field, Texas. It tells about a Army Flight Check Pilot who played a joke on one of the woman students who thought she was going to be washed out of the flying school and how she tried to kill him.

WHO STOLE THE TRAIN? This is a nonfiction semi-biographical story of an Army Officer and five soldiers racing the Russians to capture a Japanese experimental laser cannon located on a cliff overlooking the Sea of Japan during WWII. The race started in the Philippine Islands to Japan and then by Jeep to the rail line near Fujigaya Air Field where they stole a train for the run to Nikaho.

THE DIVINE WIND This is a nonfiction semibiographical story of an Army Officer who worked in the shadows during WWII. It's also about how the Kamikaze Pilots were recruited to become human bombs or terrorist. Mostly it is about how the terrorists were stopped when President Truman learned that Shinto Shrines worshiped Hachiman the God of War.

Ben & Helen 50th ANNIVERSARY Join family and friends as they celebrate the 50th Anniversary and Wedding Vow Renewal Ceremony at the Mac Dill USAF Officers Club.. 5 June 1993..

DISTINGUISHED FLYING CROSS & SILVER MEDIAL. This tells about the history of the of the DFC and is also a personal tribute to Helen M. Games who was awarded a Silver Medal for being the 86th woman in the world to fly a helicopter.

INTERVIEW OF BEN R. GAMES, PhD, MAJ, CW4 This interview was conducted by the staff of the US Navy Air Station for the Pensacola Air Museum and the DFC Society on the 29 Oct. 2008. Dr. Games received the DFC for heroism and served as a Senior Fighter Pilot for the USAF plus the INANG. He also served as a Senior Helicopter Aviator for the US Army and MIANG. Time 36 Minutes.

BEN & HELEN 67th WEDDING ANNIVERSARY. Vow and Renewal at the VFW Post 9226, Ellenton, Florida. 5 June 2010. Pictures by Errol Fletcher.

A CONSPIRACY TO RAPE AMERICA. A nonfiction story of the beginning of the Korean War until President Truman gave the command of the American forces to the United Nations. In June 1950 the name of the war was changed to the United Nations Peace Action. Fighting actually started in September 1949 and a peace treaty has never been signed. The United States agreed to abide by the United Nations Rules of War, and today US military forces can not assist in the defense of South Korea without subjecting American soldiers to being charged with war crimes.

THE CONSPIRACY TO CHANGE HISTORY. This is a History Text Book with documents, photos, pictures, letters, and medical records about three soldiers who wouldn't stop fighting the enemy during the Vietnam War. These soldiers would not surrender, and were wounded in a firefight but were not issued a purple heart medal as they were classified as not being historical casualties.

www.ingramcontent.com/pod-product-compliance
Lightning Source LLC
Chambersburg PA
CBHW052022070526
44584CB00016B/1859